Guide's Greatest

Survivor
STORIES

LORI PECKHAM, editor

BOOK CLUB

Guide's Greatest

Survivor STORIES

Pacific Press®
Publishing Association
Nampa, Idaho | www.pacificpress.com

Cover design: Brandon Reese
Cover illustration: Marcus Mashburn
Interior design: Aaron Troia

The authors assume full responsibility for the accuracy of all facts and quotations as cited in this book.

Unless otherwise noted, Scripture quotations are from THE HOLY BIBLE, NEW INTERNATIONAL VERSION®, NIV®, copyright © 1973, 1978, 1984, 2011 by Biblica, Inc.® Used by permission. All rights reserved worldwide.

Scripture quotations marked KJV are from the King James Version of the Bible.

Additional copies of this book are available for purchase by calling toll-free 1-800-765-6955 or by visiting http://www.adventistbookcenter.com.

ISBN 978-0-8163-6904-1

November 2022

Contents

Dedication

To my son, Reef. When I began editing these *Guide* book collections nineteen years ago, he was just one year old. I sat under a tree in the backyard, reading past issues in search of great stories while Reef played in the sandbox. I'd read aloud some of the most gripping ones, and even then, he'd recognize a winner. Great stories are ageless. Reef has grown up alongside "*Guide's* Greatest" and has survived his own series of adventures, for which I thank God.

Also by Lori Peckham:

Guide's Greatest Animal Stories
Guide's Greatest Brave Believer Stories
Guide's Greatest Change of Heart Stories
Guide's Greatest Discovery Stories
Guide's Greatest Faith Stories
Guide's Greatest Friendship Stories
Guide's Greatest Funny Stories
Guide's Greatest Grace Stories
Guide's Greatest Hero Stories
Guide's Greatest Hope Stories
Guide's Greatest Mischief Stories
Guide's Greatest Mission Stories
Guide's Greatest Mystery Stories
Guide's Greatest Narrow Escape Stories
Guide's Greatest Rescue Stories
Guide's Greatest Second Coming Stories
Guide's Greatest Spiritual Warfare Stories
"Insight" Presents More Unforgettable Stories
Jesus in My Shoes
Sixty Years of "Guide"

A special thanks to the authors we were unable to locate. If anyone can provide knowledge of an author's current mailing address, please relay this information to Lori Peckham, in care of Pacific Press® Publishing Association.

Preface

You are about to embark on inspiring adventures through these true stories of danger, escape, rescue, and survival. But we all know that not everyone survives the perils of a sinful planet—at least, not in the short term.

We can, however, share the confidence of the people highlighted in Hebrews 11, who lived by faith. Verse 13 reminds us, "They did not receive the things promised; they only saw them and welcomed them from a distance, admitting that they were foreigners and strangers on earth." It describes how some were imprisoned, jeered at, beaten, tortured, and even killed, but "God had planned something better for us so that only together with us would they be made perfect" (verse 40). The day will come when we will leave this earth for our heavenly home.

In the meantime, God promises this: "Never will I leave you; / never will I forsake you" (Hebrews 13:5). Jesus also assured us of His presence in His final recorded words on Earth: "Surely I am with you always, to the very end of the age" (Matthew 28:20). Those are words you can count on as you live your own exciting stories.

> "The LORD's right hand has done mighty things!
>   The LORD's right hand is lifted high;
>   the LORD's right hand has done mighty things!"
> I will not die but live,
>   and will proclaim what the LORD has done
> (Psalm 118:15–17).

The Gardener's Fortunate Mistake

by W. L. Barclay

Jean Marie," Mother called, "come quickly. Here is a surprise for you."

Jean Marie stopped what she was doing in the backyard and hurried around to the front of the house.

"What is it, Mother?" she exclaimed excitedly. Jean Marie always loved surprises.

"Hurry in the house and see what Aunt Evangeline and Uncle Howard brought for you," Mother urged.

Quickly, Jean Marie opened the door and hurried into the living room. Aunt Evangeline and Uncle Howard sat on the sofa, smiling happily as they saw the eager girl come into the room.

"Hello, Auntie; hello, Uncle," greeted Jean Marie. "I'm so glad you came over." She looked at them to see what it was they had brought, but there was nothing in sight.

Uncle and Auntie smiled at the look of expectancy on Jean Marie's face, which she tried unsuccessfully to hide.

"Come over here and sit by me," said Aunt Evangeline,

making room between herself and Uncle Howard.

Jean Marie snuggled down between them while Mother and Dad seated themselves in chairs. Aunt Evangeline reached down beside the sofa and picked up a small basket. Opening it, she reached in and took out a furry ball and placed it in Jean Marie's hands. "Just a little gift for you from Uncle and me," she said with a smile.

Her eyes large with surprise and pleasure, Jean Marie looked at the little ball of fur in her hands. It was a beautiful Siamese kitten. It looked up at her with the brightest blue eyes and meowed.

"Oh, Aunt Evangeline, how sweet of you!" cried Jean Marie. "It's just what I've always wanted. I love kitties."

She hugged the kitten to her face and thrilled at the soft touch of its fur. Because her new pet had black front paws like a pair of mittens, she named it Mittens.

The months rolled swiftly by, and every day Jean Marie would hurry home from school to play with Mittens. She was a beautiful kitten and more playful than most. She could climb like a monkey and delighted in scrambling up the curtains in the living room and bedrooms. Sometimes she would climb up the screens on the windows and hang on them and cry until someone came and helped her down to safety.

Mittens always seemed to recognize when it was time for Jean Marie to go to bed. Jean Marie liked to give her kitten a goodnight hug, but they made a game of it. When Jean Marie reached down to pick her up, Mittens would roll over out of reach, then bounce up and run under a chair or table. She would wait until Jean Marie was reaching under for her, and when her hand was almost on her, she would run under another chair or table. This would keep up for some time until the kitten finally allowed herself to be caught and hugged. Jean Marie would then feed her and go to bed. Mittens would lie down on the rug beside her bed like a faithful watchdog.

A year passed quickly, and Mittens became a full-grown cat. But she remained as cute and playful as ever.

One day Jean Marie's family moved to another house on the mission compound. Another family, the McHenrys, moved into the house that Jean Marie and her parents had vacated.

The hot summer months came, and it was time for Jean Marie's family to go to the hills for vacation. What should be done with Mittens while they were gone? Arrangements were made to leave her with one of the other mission families. Orders were given to the gardener to take Mittens to this family after Jean Marie and her parents had left for the hills.

Somehow the gardener misunderstood what he was told. So instead of taking Mittens to the family who had agreed to care for her, he took her to the house where Jean Marie had originally lived. The McHenrys had been promised a cat by someone and concluded that this was the cat. Mittens felt quite at home, for this was where she had been brought up. The family had three small children, and they enjoyed playing with her until bedtime.

The next morning they had a frightening surprise. When the mother got up, she went through the living room on the way to the kitchen and noticed something lying on the floor—something that had not been there when the family retired the night before. Wondering what it was, she stepped over to take a closer look.

She jumped back in horror. It was a cobra, a very

poisonous snake, and it was nearly three feet long!

She called for her husband, and he rushed into the room. Strangely, the cobra did not rise to spread its hood or attack them, so they ventured closer. Then they saw why the snake had not attacked them. The cobra was dead. Its head had been chewed from its body, and Mittens was sitting nearby, purring pleasantly!

The family realized what had happened. Sometime the day before, the cobra had crawled in through an open door and had hidden under a bed or in a closet. During the night, it had crawled out of its hiding place, and Mittens had found it and had attacked and killed it.

Cobras are usually afraid of cats and will run from them if possible, but this one could not get out of the house. Mittens had cleverly enticed it to strike, then, without getting bitten, had pounced on its back, grabbed it by the neck, and killed it. How thankful the family was that the snake had not bitten any of the children as they played on the floor.

Someone knocked at the door. It was the gardener. He had learned that he had made a mistake and that Mittens was to go elsewhere. The McHenrys looked at each other as the gardener took Mittens away. Then they kneeled and thanked God for His watchful care and protection in times of danger and for the fortunate mistake the gardener had made. If Mittens had not been there that night, one or more of the family might have been bitten by this poisonous snake.

And when Jean Marie returned from the hills, she was overjoyed to learn that her Mittens was a hero!

2

Jerry Learns the Hard Way

by Ellen E. Morrison

Jerry was not really a bad boy. It was just that sometimes, if he wanted to do something very much and had been told not to, he did it anyway when he thought no one was watching.

Like going to the river alone, for instance. His parents had often warned him never to go swimming alone, so he usually went with Dad or with some of his friends.

But this morning, there was no one to go with him. None of his friends were at home. He had asked Dad, but the answer was, "I'm sorry, son, but not this morning. I want to paint the garage today."

Any other time Jerry would have asked Dad to let him help with the painting. But this morning was warm and sunny, and he had his heart set on going swimming. He sat down on the front step with his little dog, Chipper, beside him.

He reached down to scratch Chipper's ear. "You know, Chipper, I'm tempted to go to the river anyway. I can swim all right, and nothing's going to happen to me."

Chipper looked up and wagged his tail as if he understood.

"You want to go too, don't you?" Jerry asked. Chipper jumped down from the step and barked joyously.

Jerry looked around the house. Dad was in the garage, stirring a can of paint. Mother was still in the kitchen. "Nobody's watching," Jerry said to Chipper. "Come on, let's go!"

Together the boy and his dog went around the other side of the house and on across the pasture. The river ran through the woods at the end of the pasture. Soon they were there, and Jerry was splashing about in the water.

There had been a lot of rain during the past few days. Jerry noticed that the river was swollen higher than usual and that the current was stronger. Yet the sight of Chipper bounding happily along the riverbank made him forget to be afraid.

Jerry decided to swim to the other side of the river, the way he and his friends often did when they were together. He struck out across the stream. At first, he didn't have any trouble. When he reached the middle of the river, however, the current became so strong that he had to fight against it. He was swimming as hard as he could but could make no headway against the swift, cold water.

Slowly, the current began sweeping him downstream. The other bank still seemed far away, and Jerry was getting tired. He would never be able to make it all the way across. Even the bank he had started from seemed far away now. Suddenly, he became very frightened and began swimming with short, choppy strokes, which wasted his strength.

Jerry's only hope now seemed to be in catching onto

something to save himself from being swept completely away by the river current. Downstream a tree branch reached out like a long arm to dip into the water. If only he could get close enough to catch it as the river carried him by!

The tree grew on the other bank, and Jerry struggled to swim a little farther across to get near the branch. Now it was right in his path as the river swept him closer. As it came to him, he reached up and grabbed with both hands. He had it! The current tried to tear him away, and the branch pulled down with his weight, but he held on.

For the first time, Jerry thought of Chipper. The dog had realized something was wrong and was now dashing back and forth along the bank Jerry had started from. Chipper stopped again and again as if he would jump in and come to Jerry.

"No, no, Chipper!" Jerry screamed above the roar of the river.

The dog paused at the spot where he had been ready to leap in. He looked across the water at his young master.

"Go get Dad!" Jerry called.

Chipper didn't move. One little ear was raised up, as if he wondered what was expected of him.

Jerry's heart sank. He had to make Chipper understand! "Go get Dad!" he called again.

Chipper stood wagging his tail furiously. Then he turned and bolted through the trees in the direction of home.

Jerry clung tightly to the sagging branch. He was shivering now and getting colder every minute. The angry river tugged at him constantly. If only he could hold on long enough! If only Chipper could make Dad come! He looked fearfully up at the branch, hoping it wouldn't crack under his added weight.

Every moment seemed an hour to Jerry. What if Chipper hadn't understood after all and was playing somewhere on the way home? He was afraid to think of that.

Then he heard a welcome shout. "Jerry! Where are you?" his father called.

"Here I am!" Jerry shouted as loudly as he could.

Dad, with Chipper at his heels, came through the trees at the riverbank and looked out over the water. He had a long rope in his hand.

"Here, Dad!" Jerry cried. He was so weak now he felt as if he would let go at any moment.

Then his father saw him. "Hold on, Jerry!" he shouted. "I'll throw the rope to you."

Dad quickly tied one end of the rope to a tree. Then he poised on the bank and threw the rest of the rope toward his son. It fell short and floated past Jerry. Dad pulled the rope in quickly and threw it again. This time it went almost across the river, and the current carried it swiftly down to where Jerry clung to the tree branch. Before it could pass him, Jerry grabbed it with one hand.

"Hold tight!" his father shouted.

Jerry flipped the rope till it was around his wrist. Then he let go of the branch and quickly grasped the rope with his second hand as the current swept him downstream. The rope tightened with a jerk, and he felt himself pulled toward the shore. Soon he was close enough to catch the hand Dad reached out to him.

"Thanks, Dad," Jerry chattered, trying to stop shivering.

"That was a close call, son," his father said. "Here, take my coat and put it around you."

Jerry was thankful for the warm coat, and he remembered to give faithful little Chipper a loving hug. Then he and Dad started home, with Chipper romping ahead. Dad had not said a word about why Jerry had come to the river alone.

Jerry reached up timidly to put his hand through his father's arm. "I'm sorry, Dad," he said.

"That's all right, son," Dad replied, looking down at him with a smile and patting his hand.

And it really was all right. They both knew that Jerry had learned a lesson the hard way. He would not disobey again, even when he thought no one was watching.

3

The Guardian Angel of Summer Camp

by Harold E. Haas

Hey, Johnnie, wake up!" Frank shook his friend's shoulder. "See, the sun is shining, and it looks like we'll be able to take that long boat ride Elder Smith promised us."

Frank wasn't the only excited boy that morning. All the juniors at Louisiana's summer camp were eagerly looking forward to the boat ride the camp director, Elder Smith, had promised. But there had been so much rain that it had to be postponed.

Today looked like the perfect weather for a boat ride around the lake! It would take about four hours, leading them beneath hanging Spanish moss and through trails cut in the cypress trees that grew right up out of the water. They would go back into the secret parts of the lake that, so far, they had seen only from a distance.

Soon the entire camp was awake, and everyone was talking about the boat ride. In the showers, at the breakfast table, in the kitchen, all the campers chattered about that one thing.

"I can hardly wait until ten o'clock when we're to start on the boat ride," said one camper.

"Neither can I," came the answer. "I'm so excited I don't know what to do."

"I wonder what we'll see," piped in another junior. "Maybe there will be an alligator!"

"Oh, wouldn't that be thrilling," said a girl. "Hurry up, ten o'clock!"

The sun did come out bright and early that Thursday morning. But around nine thirty, rain clouds gathered, and the sky grew gray and dark. Shadows were soon reflected in the faces of the campers, for they feared the rain might rob them of the trip.

But frowns changed to smiles when Elder Smith announced that everyone should put on a swimming suit, for the boat ride would go on as scheduled, rain or shine.

There was a deafening cheer of approval. Campers raced to their cabins, changed into their swimming suits, and marched back to the lake.

"Look," shouted Frank. "Here come the boats!"

Rounding the bend in the lake, eight boats appeared, tied one behind the other, pulled by a motor in front. Fourteen more boats were in another string, pulled by a funny-looking barge with two long blades reaching out in front to cut weeds and trash from the lake.

In just a matter of minutes, the campers were loading in.

"Only four juniors, one counselor, and a life preserver to a boat," Elder Smith said.

The boats were loaded with such caution that some of the juniors became impatient.

"You must sit perfectly still," Elder Smith told them when all were aboard. "There must be no foolishness whatsoever. We can't take any chances of an accident spoiling our fun."

Then, at last, they were off.

Frank and Johnnie were in the first boat behind the barge with the long, sharp blades.

"Isn't this just about the most fun you ever had in all your life?" said Frank.

"It certainly is!" agreed Johnnie. "I'm so glad I came to camp this year. I'm not going to miss a single one until I pass the age limit."

There were so many interesting things to see! They spotted huge masses of fish eggs on the bottom of the lake as well as egrets, graceful birds with long legs and long necks. They also passed beautiful trees and the trailing Spanish moss. But there were no alligators.

Perhaps it would have been better if the most dangerous thing that had happened had been seeing an alligator. What nearly injured some of them that day had teeth much sharper than an alligator's and just as deadly.

About two-thirds of the way around the lake, something went wrong with the little barge that was pulling the first string of boats. It stopped and appeared to be having trouble. All eyes fixed on the two men the Park Commission had sent to run the barge.

Rumors began to fly thick and fast. "Probably ran out of gas!" said Betty.

"More than likely, we got water in the carburetor," guessed one of the boys.

"I wonder if we'll have to swim back," said one of the little girls.

"I hope it doesn't start to rain again while we're stuck here," said another.

One of the older girls in another boat started to shout a question to Frank in the front boat. She stood up, but Elder Smith saw her. "Keep your seat," he called over. "They'll have the barge going in a few minutes, I'm sure."

The girl subsided into her chair again. But she cupped her hands to her lips and shouted, "Frank, can you see what the trouble is?"

Frank shouted back, "I just heard one of the men say the barge is sinking."

"Oh no!" gasped several of the girls at once. "How will we ever get home?"

"What fun," commented some boys. "We'll be able to sit out here till they send for another barge to haul us back."

But just then, the other man who was driving the barge turned to the campers. "Don't worry," he said, smiling. "The barge isn't going to sink. It can't. It's unsinkable."

The words had hardly left his mouth, however, when it became evident that, sinkable or unsinkable, the barge was surely sinking! And it was sinking fast. A stump on the bottom of the lake, which no one had seen, had gouged a hole in it, and water was pouring in.

"Quick!" shouted an alert counselor. "Johnnie and Frank, untie the chain that holds the barge to the rest of the boats so the barge won't drag us down with it."

As quickly as they could, they untied the chain. But fast as they were, they were none too fast, for just as they finished, the barge, like a dying fish, began to roll over.

Up to this moment, everyone had been worrying about the motor. They had forgotten all about those long, sharp blades in front of the barge that cut through the trash and rubbish in the water.

But now, suddenly, one of those blades was towering

above a boat full of girls. It hovered for an instant, like an arm with a dagger, ready to strike a death blow.

"Help!" screamed the littlest girl in the boat as she saw the danger. But there was no way to help them. There was no way to move the boat and nowhere to run.

Campers and counselors in the other boats cringed. They turned their eyes away, afraid to see what would happen next. The director's face grew pale.

"Please, God," gasped Frank, "please, do something to help them, quick!"

Closer came that cruel blade, its sharp teeth seeming eager to hurt those poor girls. The counselor in the boat grabbed one of the girls and shoved her into the bottom of the boat. Then, as the blade grew even closer, the counselor threw up an arm, as if, with her bare hands, she would push away the cruel monster.

And it was then that the angels intervened. For just at the moment everyone was sure the girls were going to be hurt, that great blade stopped, turned, and fell harmlessly into the water at the boat's side.

It had all happened so quickly that the campers hardly realized it. Many found themselves trembling from the fright. The color returned to the director's face. "Thank You, God," whispered Frank. And the two men from the Park Commission hitched up all the boats in one line—twenty-two in a row—and started the journey back.

Camp was over all too soon. The last goodbyes were said, and everyone promised to "see you next year." The director walked down to the lakeshore and gazed across the water where death's angel had come so close. And then, seeing he was alone, he talked out loud to himself. "When I think what a large number of boys and girls come to

Seventh-day Adventist summer camps every year, and how few of them ever get hurt," he said, "I am convinced that the guardian angel comes to summer camp too."

4

The Hungry Coyotes

by Thelma Lee Olander

Martha Truitt knew that if she lived a hundred years, she would never forget that awful summer when the grasshoppers came. They ate every green thing in the field, prairie, garden, and orchard.

Mr. and Mrs. Truitt, with their two boys and one girl, had come to Kansas with other pioneers to make a home where they could get free land. Breaking the sod and planting crops had not been easy, but everyone worked, and there had always been food for the winter. But this year, it would be different.

In August, after the wheat had been harvested, there was promise of a large corn crop. The apple and peach trees were bending with the weight of fruit, and the summer gardens were green. Then came the glittering hordes of grasshoppers, and when August was over, there was nothing left. Even the leaves on the trees were gone.

Mrs. Truitt was a brave, godly woman. She taught her children to pray, and in the wild, lonely country where they lived, a sense of God's presence was very real to them. No problem was too small to take to their best Friend. Somehow they knew He would see them through the long winter ahead.

One afternoon in late December, Mrs. Truitt said to twelve-year-old Martha, "I must bake bread tomorrow, and my yeast has spoiled. Father and the boys won't be in from chopping wood until almost dark, and then it will be too late to go to Mrs. Bryson's to borrow some. You must go right away so you can get back before dark."

Out on the plains, there were no grocery stores where she might buy bread or even yeast cakes. Women baked their own bread and saved a little of the batter from each batch to start the next baking. Sometimes the yeast spoiled, and then a neighbor would borrow "starter yeast" from another woman.

As Martha took her coat from its hook, Mother continued, "The days are so short now; it won't be long until dark. You must hurry there and back. Father says the coyotes are running in packs, and they are much worse after dark. Wear your heavy boots, too, for it looks like snow."

Mr. and Mrs. Bryson, the Truitts' nearest neighbors, lived two miles away. The rutted wagon road ran through a thicket of trees, then out onto the open prairie, over a large hill, and down into a ravine where a stream laughed and played in the summer. Today it was tightly frozen, and Martha gave in to the temptation to slide a little on the smooth ice. But she hurried up the last hill to the Brysons' sod house.

She visited a little time with friendly Mrs. Bryson. Then, noticing snowflakes falling, she said, "I must be going. It's beginning to snow, and I'm afraid it will be dark before I get home."

Mrs. Bryson fixed the dish of yeast so it could be easily carried and said, "Before you go, I want to give you a package of food."

"Oh, that is kind of you. We haven't had much to eat this winter, for the grasshoppers didn't leave anything. Father saved some of our potatoes and carrots."

Mrs. Bryson handed Martha a large parcel, helped her fasten her coat, and warned her to be careful. The wind was cold, and the sharp spikes of snow felt like tiny pieces of glass as they hit the girl's cheeks, but she thought of the good meals they would have the next several days. Mother would know how to make that extra food stretch as far as possible.

Martha hurried down the hill to the little ravine, but she didn't stop to slide on the tempting ice now. The cold, gray day would soon be over, and she must be home before dark.

As she hurried along, she heard a faint *awoo-o-o!* It seemed to come from up the ravine.

"Coyotes!" whispered the girl in fright. "Father said they were running in packs! I must hurry!" But with the large package of food and the round dish of yeast, it was almost impossible to run. She walked along as briskly as she could.

Then there came another *awoo-o-o-o-o* much closer.

Martha broke into a clumsy run. The road was rough, and with the heavy bundle and the smooth dish of yeast, she couldn't run very far at a time. Her breath was coming in short gasps, and the cold air tore at her throat.

She glanced behind her, and the sight she saw made her tremble with fear! Six or seven coyotes were following her about fifty yards behind, sniffing the air hungrily.

"The food! They smell my food. Oh, what shall I do!"

Food was scarce, and Martha had no intention of throwing her package away. But neither did she care to be attacked by the coyotes.

As she entered the dim thicket of trees, she could hear the animals coming closer. They were cautious but unafraid, as they seemed to sense there was strength in their numbers. If only Father and the boys knew of her danger, they would come to her aid, but they would not be able to hear her if she called.

"Jesus can help you!" Out of her fear, she seemed to hear the words.

"Oh, dear Jesus," she prayed, "please help me! I am so afraid!"

"Drop some of the food." It seemed a voice had spoken to her, and quickly, she reached into the package, grabbed some of the food, and hurled it with all her might at the pack of slinking coyotes. Then with fear giving wings to her feet, she fairly flew along the frozen, snow-covered road.

The suddenness of her action surprised the animals. As they pounced upon the food, snarling and fighting among themselves, the delay gave her time to reach her own yard.

As she stumbled into the one room of their little sod house, Mother looked up from the meal she was preparing. Martha's face was white with fear, and her breath came in short, painful gasps, but she still held the precious package of food and the dish of yeast.

When Martha showed Mother what Mrs. Bryson had given her and told her of the coyotes, her fear, her prayer, and the voice she had heard, Mrs. Truitt went to the shelf where she kept her big Bible. She opened it to Psalm 91. She began at the first verse and read the entire psalm to the girl huddled in the big rocking chair. When she reached the fourteenth and fifteenth verses, she read them slowly and with feeling: "Because he hath set his love upon me, therefore will I deliver him. . . . He shall call upon me, and I will answer him: I will be with him in trouble; I will deliver him" (KJV).

"Martha," said her mother, "never forget this day. Always set your love upon Him, and when you call, He will answer."

5

Angel in the Storm

by Jan S. Doward

When storms come to Nushagak Bay in southwestern Alaska, they come with a fury that is next to a typhoon. Eighty-mile-an-hour winds sometimes whip the sea to froth and endanger every fisherman and fisherwoman in the muddy bay. Because the bay is so shallow, it is rougher than most other places when storms strike—and they usually do in the fishing season.

During one of the worst storms on record in Nushagak Bay, Tommy and his companion found themselves in peril. They had been fishing for several hours when they received a storm warning over their shortwave. Bringing in their nets, they headed for shore.

But before they could reach safety, the sea became one vast, churning mass of treacherous motion. The water and sky met in a dismal gray that blotted visibility. Their boat bobbed and tossed, fighting to gain shelter. And it was taking on water fast. Soon it would be completely swamped.

"Bail hard!" Tommy cried to his friend.

But the harder they bailed, the more water came in. They had sprung a leak in the aft part of the boat, and it seemed that the whole bay was about to rush upon them as some mighty monster to its prey. Working as they had never worked before, the two exhausted themselves in an effort to keep the boat afloat.

"If we swamp and turn over in this storm," shouted Tommy, "the mast will stick in the mud, and we'll be lost."

He was right. The bay was so shallow in that part that the mast would stick in the mud. Yet the water was too deep to wade to safety. To swim would be impossible in the storm, and land was so far away that it was out of sight. They would never be seen if their boat capsized. Alone and stuck, they would perish in the cold, relentless waves of the Nushagak.

Tommy was sure it would help matters if he were to throw the mast away. But he couldn't get it loose, and that was the first time he prayed. "Oh, God, help me get the mast off!"

He worked as he prayed, but it seemed that with every effort to turn the wrench and twist on the nuts, he had less strength. The nuts were corroded and would not come loose. Drenched to the skin and weary from the struggle, he prayed again that God would help him remove the mast from its base before the next wave tipped the boat over. The boat gave a lurch that sent Tommy sprawling, but he was back again, trying with every ounce of energy left.

"If—if only it would come off," he muttered. The salt spray stung his eyes, the rain soaked him, but still he worked on.

His companion bailed and bailed water but finally called for help. "Let the mast go, and help back here!"

Going to the back of the boat, Tommy grabbed a bailing can, but just then, something very strange happened. Forward—right by the mast—why, it was the mast moving! The wind wasn't blowing it over, or it would have fallen rapidly. Slowly, it lifted from its base and gradually toppled into the foaming sea as if some giant hand had picked it up and put it there.

In amazement, the two watched from the stern, but just as this happened, it seemed the world went topsy-turvy. Rolling up a high crest, the little fishing boat tilted crazily for a moment, then flipped completely over.

The two young men leaped for their lives. Coming to the surface, they floundered about until they caught the sides of their boat.

"It's the end," gasped Tommy's companion.

All too well Tommy knew what a capsized boat in the Nushagak meant. They would never be found until the storm was over, and by then, they would have drowned. Sometimes it is not possible to make any rescues for ten days.

Clinging to the side of the boat, they pitched and tossed, up and down. The raging storm had not subsided at all. An hour went by. Two hours.

Tommy's companion was so weak he had to be supported. With his arm around his friend and looking up toward heaven, Tommy prayed that God would send help. Hadn't He sent an angel to take the mast down? Surely God would not let them die out here in the bitterly cold Nushagak.

"I—I can't—I just can't hang on any longer," his companion gasped.

Tommy pulled on his friend's shoulder, trying to give

him strength, trying desperately to help him hang on.

The incessant waves beat against the sides of the boat and jerked them unmercifully. Tommy knew the end was near. They could not stay in the water much longer. Gathering strength for one last effort, he pleaded with his companion to cling tightly while he prayed once more. Leaving him, Tommy worked his way around the side of the boat and forced himself up on the overturned stern. There he knelt and, for the last time, asked God to send aid.

As he prayed, a text came to his mind that he had recently learned in Sabbath School: "The angel of the LORD encampeth round about them that fear him, and delivereth them" (Psalm 34:7, KJV). If ever they needed to be delivered, it was now. If ever they needed one of God's strong angels, it was now.

Then somehow, it happened. Tommy could not believe his eyes at first because things like this do not just happen, especially in the midst of a storm on the Nushagak. Another fishing boat was coming straight for them, right out of the mist. A boat—a real boat to the rescue!

Tommy and his companion were picked up by the friendly rescue boat and taken to safety. Their boat was gone, the nets and fish were gone, and it seemed that everything was lost. But these two young men were glad to be alive and, most of all, glad that they had seen the power of a prayer-answering God. They would never forget that God knows how to answer the prayers of His children when they are in need and that He sends His angels into the storm.

6

Hidden by the Angels

by Lawrence Maxwell

Right in the middle of Sabbath School, the door to the children's division opened. An angry-looking woman came in waving a knife.

"Where's Wanda?" she demanded.

The young people were too frightened to answer. Finally, one of the Sabbath School teachers said, "Wanda isn't in this division."

"I'm going to find her!" the angry woman shouted. "She said she's going to be baptized, but no daughter of mine is ever going to be baptized in this church!"

The angry woman stalked around the room, looking for her daughter. But Wanda was not to be found. The woman gave up and hurried to the adult division.

Wanda and her best friend, Lila, lived in a heathen village. But when they heard about Sabbath School at the Adventist mission, they decided to go. Their mothers weren't pleased, but they didn't stop the girls.

At Sabbath School, Wanda and Lila heard about Jesus

and His wonderful love. It wasn't long before a deep desire sprang up in their hearts to be baptized.

The day for the baptism was set, and all the arrangements were made. Wanda and Lila were very happy. They told their mothers, but their mothers weren't happy at all. Wanda's mother actually threatened to kill her if she got baptized! What should the girls do? It was a tremendous decision, and they were only fifteen years old. Should they risk their lives to follow Jesus?

Wanda knew what she was going to do, and Lila said the same. They were going to follow Jesus no matter the cost.

So, on Sabbath morning, they went to Sabbath School prepared for the baptismal service. And true to her word, Wanda's mother came a few minutes later, prepared for what she intended to do. That's why she walked into the Sabbath School room with a knife in her hand.

But Wanda and Lila were in the adult division. And there was no way to hide them. They were sitting in the front row!

The two girls saw Wanda's mother enter. They saw the huge knife in her hand, and they knew what it was for.

Everyone sat perfectly still while the mother walked up and down the aisles, waving her weapon, searching for her daughter. They heard her shout, "Where is Wanda?" They saw her look right at the two girls. And they saw her leave.

The two girls had been sitting in plain sight, but Wanda's mother had not seen them. Surely God sent His angels that day to protect those two girls who were willing to risk their lives because they loved Him.

7

Larry Races a Locomotive!

by Nellia Burman Garber

It had been a delightful afternoon. The entire Simms family had enjoyed every moment of it. The crisp air of the pine-clad mountains, the smoke-flavored food cooked over the open fire, the joy of being together—no one could say which they had enjoyed the most. But each had that snug feeling that goes with complete contentment.

Very little was being said as the car sped down the mountain slopes. Mr. Simms guessed the children must have eaten so much they couldn't talk. Mrs. Simms thought it was because they were all so tired from the long hike to the top of the ridge. But the children didn't care about the reasons. They were just content to sit and stare idly at the scenery flying by.

"We're almost home," Tom observed as his father began to slow down from the first descent. "I hope we arrive in time to play awhile."

"I think we'll be home before dark, son," his father answered. "Of course, there are a few chores to be done too."

"Leave it to Dad to bring that up," said Larry with a laugh. "As if we could forget!"

"Dad wouldn't let us," teased Tom.

Just then, Mrs. Simms noticed a look of concern cross her husband's face. She didn't ask him what was wrong because she didn't want to upset the boys. But she watched his face closely to try to figure out what the trouble might be. Then she knew; it was the brakes. She saw him push the brake pedal clear to the floor, but the car moved along without a sign of stopping. Fear clutched her heart. What if they had to stop and couldn't?

Both parents were glad they weren't in city traffic, where they would need to stop for signal lights. But at the same time, they longed for a service station. There was none in sight, for they had already turned onto the farm road.

Little by little, Mr. Simms allowed the car to lose momentum, then kept it at as even a pace as possible with his hand on the gear. The trouble was that the car had one of the earlier-model automatic gears, and it was much harder to control a runaway car with it than with a manual transmission.

"Going mighty slow, aren't we?" Tom commented, still thinking of the game and the few precious moments of evening left for it.

"Going plenty fast enough, son," his father replied. Then he told the boys that the brake fluid had leaked out and suggested they pray to God to give them extra protection.

Scarcely had he asked the boys to pray when the car turned a curve in the road, and they saw a train track about a half mile ahead. Mrs. Simms looked at her watch. She knew exactly when the train passed at that crossing, for the family had lived within hearing distance of the line for years. That glimpse of her watch confirmed her fears—it was train time.

"Oh, God," she prayed silently, "let the train be late today." But even before she had finished her prayer, she heard the train whistle.

"Pray, pray," said Mr. Simms fervently.

It was easy to see why. At the rate the car was going, they would be carried right in front of the locomotive. There was nothing he could do about it. To accelerate and try to beat the train would be sheer folly. Yet he couldn't hope that the train would pass before the car rolled onto the track.

The train's roar never sounded so loud as it did that day. The family could almost feel the wheels passing over them. Once more Father begged, "Pray!" and pushed on the dead brake with all his might.

With a grab that nearly sent Mr. and Mrs. Simms through the windshield, the brakes took a firm hold. The car stopped just a few feet from the path of the steel monster!

The feeling of deliverance left the family weak and shaken but happy that God had worked a miracle for their safety.

"Oh," someone might say, "the fluid just got into the lines again." No, for after the car had crossed the track, again the brakes didn't work, and Father had to creep along until they came to a filling station.

The angels applied those brakes. The car didn't just stop. Ask Larry. He told me the story himself, and he is thoroughly convinced that it was not his father who applied the brakes that afternoon. He says it was the same hand that closed the ark and shut the lions' mouths for Daniel.

8

Charlie and the Writhing Monster

by Josephine Cunnington Edwards

There was something strange about the hot weather that day. Once in a while, a breeze unbelievably cool elbowed its way into the heat and sultriness. I hardly knew what to make of it.

I was all alone in our second-floor apartment in Minneapolis. It was time to set up tents for camp meeting at Anoka, and my husband and Charlie, our twelve-year-old son, were there working hard.

With the family away, I had some time to call my own. The little apartment was clean. I had a story I wanted to write, so I had found a pile of paper and some sharpened pencils and was sitting where I could get a breeze while I wrote.

Then the phone rang. It was my husband calling from Anoka.

"Jo?"

"Yes. Anything wrong?"

"Could you come out to Anoka today and stay here?"

"Anything the matter?"

"No, only we are lonesome for you, and they want you to cook for the workers' camp, and we are being slowly eaten alive with mosquitoes."

I agreed to go out there and fix up the tent and cook for the camp and put up the mosquito nets.

I packed the car with all the things I thought we would need. I took box after box down to the car and was glad I had washed that morning. Soon the car was loaded with curtains folded neatly, nets, bedspreads, sheets, quilts, rugs, a few dishes, a hot plate, some kettles, and a few canned things so we could have little camp meals after the meetings began.

On the way out of town, I stopped at a service station to get gas.

"Strange weather, ain't it?" the friendly attendant remarked. "My father says it's tornado weather."

I had never lived in a place where we had such things, as I was new to Minnesota. Such talk was terrifying. I inquired further, a little disturbed.

"Is there such a thing as tornado weather?" I asked.

"Oh, yes," the man replied. "See, a tornado is a storm that sort of gets to whirlin' 'round when the wind blows hot and cold like it is today. Pa says that's a sure way to get a tornado started."

After that cheerful prophecy, I got on my way to the campground at Anoka. Most of the time, the heat was overpowering. Then a cooling breeze would come in and fan my face surprisingly. It was as if a door had been opened briefly to a giant's icebox.

I drove down the shady block to the entrance of the lovely park where the camp meeting was held for years in

Minnesota. Charlie spotted me immediately. He ran to the car, overjoyed to see me. He immediately asked if I'd brought anything to eat, especially cookies. Then he said, "Boy, is it hot! See how I'm sweating? That's because I'm helping Dad and Elder Lidner. They're putting up tents." He got into the car and directed me to where our tent was.

While he helped me unload, he smiled broadly at the big mosquito net. "Am I glad you brought that!" he declared. "The mosquitoes almost ate us up last night."

We started to work to fix the tent. In the front part, we made a small living room, with chairs and cushions and a table. A folding cot with a bright blanket and a colorful rug on the floor made it an attractive place.

But when we got ready to put up the divider curtains and mosquito nets, I was disgusted with myself. I'd brought neither a hammer nor any tacks.

"There's nothing to do but go into town and buy some tacks and pins," I said. "I can't do another thing until we have them."

I stepped out of the tent to go to the car and ran into Brother Hiatt, who was, for many years, the educational secretary of the conference. He soon found out about my problem and sent Charlie to get a hammer while he went back to his own tent for the extra box of tacks he declared he had.

I am alive today because Elder Hiatt had that extra box of tacks. Instead of going along that road in the car, I was busy with my curtains when I heard people shouting. I went outside, and Charlie came running to me, his face white with fear.

"A tornado, Mother! A tornado!"

We ran to where a group of workers was standing and

watching the dreadful sight of the twister coming across the open prairie right toward us. The sound was like a sawmill going crazy, like a thousand express trains, like heartbeats pulsing in a terrible rhythm of death. The air smelled brassy and odd, and then, for a minute, it seemed as if there were no air at all—nothing to breathe.

The cloud in the sky had grown round, with a rim of yellowish gray like mildew. It was coming fast toward us. It was a writhing monster; its tail like a giant python, rolling and twisting and destroying like a mighty rope of death. The twisting fury and strength of that rope pulled up mighty oaks as if they were carrots in a rain-soaked garden. Houses and barns and sheds and trees were sucked up into the terrible vortex and were flying above our very heads now, whirling and rolling. I wondered how soon it would be till we would be up there, being destroyed by this frightful fury.

My husband and Charlie and I sought shelter in our car.

"Will we die, Mother; will we die?" Charlie asked me.

"I think so," I told him.

His mouth was close to my ear. "How long do we have to live?" he asked.

"Maybe three minutes. Maybe less," I said.

We knelt down in that small space between the seats and prayed. Silly cherished sins seemed so trivial in that hour when, at any moment, we were expecting death. I never heard a sweeter prayer than Charlie prayed those few pulsating moments when we believed death was imminent. He asked the Lord to forgive us of our sins, and he asked for Him to grant us the gift of another life—an eternal life with Him forever.

It was strange, but in those dreadful moments, we didn't feel fear. That came later. We were very calm, and we had the comforting feeling that all would be well, no matter what way the thing went.

Our prayers over, we peered out of the car. The noise was so deafening we couldn't hear one another speak. The writhing tail was almost upon us.

Suddenly—only God knows how it happened—the dreadful thing turned and started the other way. It went right along the very road I would have been taking had I gone to get the tacks. Down that crowded road it went, sucking up cars, people, animals, trees. The hundreds of tiny tents stood untouched. Not one of them was blown down. But the town of Anoka lay in ruins from the fury of the storm.

That evening we had reason to thank God, not only for our little tented city but for our very lives. Not a mile away were desolation and destruction that would take years to rebuild. As we went to our little dwelling tent, the three of us knelt and rededicated our lives to the service of the Lord.

9

Lawrence and the Open Door

by Goldie Down

You should shut your door, sahib. It isn't safe to have open doors," one of Lawrence's friends told him. They called him *sahib*—a term Indians use to address a European respectfully.

Lawrence laughed. He had spent some time selling books in India before becoming a schoolteacher. He believed he knew how to take care of himself—even in a foreign country.

"Too hot," he replied to the Indian friends who were so gravely advising him to keep the door of his bungalow shut. "Much too hot. I like plenty of fresh air, especially when I have to do my own cooking."

"But, sahib, you are living on the outskirts of town," another friend pointed out. "It is not safe here."

"At least shut the door before dusk," a third piped in.

"Oh, of course." Lawrence chuckled. "I always keep my door closed at night. It lets in too many mosquitoes otherwise. Don't worry; I can look after myself."

As his Indian friends reluctantly left, Lawrence continued to chuckle. "Very cautious lot, these people. Scared of their own shadows. All the windows barred and doors locked. Not very fond of fresh air, either." Lawrence shook his head and turned to prepare his lessons for the next day, dismissing the matter from his mind.

Then one late afternoon, Lawrence was preparing his supper and studying at the same time. His books were open on the kitchen table, and as he read, he kept an eye on the pot bubbling on the little stove. He had only one small burner, and it took a long time to prepare a meal.

Lawrence jumped to his feet as the sizzling sound of rice water spilling into the fire roused him. Expertly, he whipped the lid off the boiling pot and fished out a few grains of rice. He tested them between a finger and thumb. "They're cooked," he murmured. "Now I'll make a curry." He set the rice aside to cool.

In no time at all, Lawrence had peeled onions and potatoes and had them frying in a mixture of oil and pungent spices. He considered himself a good cook, and he was proud of his ability to make a tasty curry. He licked his lips in anticipation and turned back to his books.

Soon he was deep in his reading, elbows resting on the table and chin resting in his cupped hands. So absorbed was he that he did not see or hear anything but the merry spitting in the frying pan.

He did not stir until something lightly brushed against his cheek. He turned his head and looked right into the green eyes of a tiger that was sniffing at his left ear!

Lawrence froze as cold terror seized him in its grip. For a split second, his mind stood still, and then his thoughts raced frantically in search of a solution. Schoolteacher that he was, he had never faced a problem like this before. What did one do when one discovered a tiger breathing down the back of one's neck? No textbook he had ever read mentioned such a situation.

The tiger's whiskers brushed Lawrence's left cheek as it sniffed the back of his neck. Lawrence sat as still as if he were one piece with the chair. But his anguished mind was seeking aid. *Help, God. Oh, help me,* his brain implored. *I can do nothing. No weapon. No person within hearing. God, did I come to India to become a tiger's dinner? Help me. Oh, help.*

In answer to his prayer, the tiger stopped sniffing his neck and padded slowly toward the pan of frying vegetables. Its head thrust forward; it sniffed inquisitively at the curry. The steam rising from the pan was hot to its nose, and the tiger drew back quickly and looked at Lawrence reproachfully, as if to say, "Why didn't you tell me it was hot?"

But Lawrence was too frightened to stir. As if mesmerized, he watched the tiger take another step and cautiously sniff at the pot of cooling rice. Finding it not too hot, the tiger hungrily thrust its face into the pot and licked up the food. When the last grain was devoured, the tiger raised its head, licked all around its mouth with a giant pink tongue, then glanced appreciatively at Lawrence and nodded as if to say, "Thanks, pal."

For the first time in his life, Lawrence was praying with his eyes open, watching the tiger's every move. *Oh, God, save me. Help me. Make it go outside.*

The tiger was now exploring the little kitchen, sniffing here and there and eyeing Lawrence speculatively, as if wondering whether he would make a good dessert.

Finding there was nothing else to eat, the tiger paused

a moment, then padded toward the table. Its face loomed larger and larger as it came nearer and nearer until it filled the whole of Lawrence's vision. He thought surely his end had come when the tiger sniffed at his right cheek. His frantic prayers reached a crescendo of fear as stories of man-eaters flashed through his mind. At any minute, he expected to be seized in those mighty jaws and have his neck broken with a single blow.

The tiger sniffed again. Lawrence's heart stopped beating and then raced with hope as the tiger slowly, almost reluctantly, padded toward the door.

As its tail disappeared over the threshold, Lawrence came to life. With one mighty leap, he reached the door and slammed it shut. He shot home the big bolt and stood trembling with his back to the door. But in that position, he was facing the open, unbarred window. What if the tiger should come in the window?

Lawrence's heart began to pound again. Would the tiger . . . He waited breathlessly for the striped head to appear at the opening, but nothing happened. The tiger had gone. His prayers had been answered.

It has been many years since Lawrence retired from his work in India, but I am sure he has never forgotten the day he almost became a tiger's dinner.

10

Trap for Shirley

by Bonnie Burgeson

S hirley trudged along in the gathering darkness. She quickened her footsteps for two reasons. First, she could hardly wait to get to her best friend's house. She and Louise always had so much fun together. The second reason was because she felt uneasy about being alone in this desolate part of the big city at this time of the evening.

She whistled a tune to give herself courage. *Just seven more blocks, then five more blocks, and finally three more blocks to go!* she thought.

Most of the way, streetlights had illuminated her path, but now she was coming to a dark section. Ahead of her stretched six railroad tracks to be crossed and then a long, old-fashioned bridge over a large creek. On the right side, at the end of the bridge, she could see a high stone wall that extended to the end of the block. On the left side was a seldom-used road that followed the creek.

Shirley had almost reached the first railroad tracks when a car shone its lights full on her—a thirteen-year-old girl walking alone in this lonely place. The car drove past her and stopped, turned completely around, and drove back to the end of the stone wall. It then turned around again, came back to the bridge, and backed into the seldom-used road with its front end as close to the exit of the bridge as possible. Then its lights went off.

By this time, Shirley had crossed all six railroad tracks and was about to enter the bridge. She sensed a feeling of danger. She knew a trap had been set for her. This car could easily drive forward and block her exit from the bridge. She had come too far to go back now, though. Breathing a silent prayer to God for protection, she crossed the road to walk on the other side of the bridge from where the car was parked.

Right then, she heard someone behind her. She whirled around, trembling.

A tall, attractive woman greeted Shirley with a smile. "Hello," she said as she began to cross the bridge beside Shirley.

Soon they were almost across from the dark, silent parked car. Shirley glanced in its direction. Just as they left the bridge, the car turned on its lights, started its motor— but the motor died! The beam of the car's headlights revealed not the lone girl who had entered the bridge but a tall woman and a husky bulldog walking between Shirley and the car. The woman kept on walking with Shirley and visiting with her until they passed the long stone wall and arrived at Louise's house.

Shirley didn't see where this woman came from or where she went, and she didn't learn her name. But she had a good idea. Shirley, my mother, believes she met her guardian angel that night.

11

Two Hundred Hooves Against Two Girls

by Robert G. Natiuk

Teddy wasn't the handsomest, strongest dog you've ever seen. His bright gold-and-brown fur had faded, as if he had taken a bath in a tub of bleach. His ears hung down in a pathetic sort of way. And if you had looked closely into his lusterless eyes, you would have noticed that he didn't see very much, for he was almost blind.

On the other hand, Diane, one of his owners, was a tumbling tomboy. At three years old, she was full of bounce, jump, climb, and run. She had to herself a world of grass, trees, hills, and fields, and she intended to enjoy them all.

Right after dinner one Sabbath, Diane said to her sister, Louise, "Please take me for a walk."

Louise was fourteen and liked nature hikes. But she also liked to tease. "And why should I take you for a walk?"

Diane brushed the hair out of her eyes, jumped out of her chair, and gave her big sister a big hug to match. " 'Cause there are flowers in the pasture and new baby calves. Mama says I can't see them if you don't come along." Diane tugged at Louise's hand.

Their neighbor, Mr. Regg, kept some of the most beautiful Aberdeen Angus cattle in Ontario, Canada. And they had recently birthed calves.

Louise opened the kitchen door. "What are we waiting for, little sis? Beat you to the fence!" She pretended to hurry.

Diane bounded down the steps and dashed across the yard to the pasture fence. Louise was right behind her, pretending to be running with all her might and making Diane giggle happily.

Old Teddy creaked up till he was in a standing position on his favorite sleeping place by the porch. He heard the girls, and after a long stretch, he loped slowly after them.

Diane was already crawling under the fence. Louise climbed over, and Teddy got down on his forelegs and inched under. Even though he was old, he still liked to romp with the girls. Maybe he thought he'd better be around to take good care of them also.

"Oh, look!" Diane screamed with glee, bouncing up and down like a rubber ball. "There are the baby calves! Oh, they're pretty!"

Several calves were toddling beside their mothers. The older cows eyed the girls and dog suspiciously.

The girls were used to the cattle and felt no reason to be afraid. Then Louise noticed that a few seemed unusually restless and wagged their heads. The mother cows were watching every move the old dog made.

"I'd better carry you." Louise lifted Diane for a piggyback ride. She started walking around the herd, but she didn't get far.

A cow bawled loudly, and others joined in. Louise saw

Teddy walk close to the cows. He barked at them throatily. One cow staged a mock attack on the old dog, running up to him with head lowered and stopping a foot away.

Teddy ran in small circles, barking wildly. Perhaps he thought the girls were in danger.

"Stop it, Teddy! Go home!" Louise shouted at him. But the dog only barked more loudly.

The cattle began milling around, stamping, pawing, bawling. Louise dared not move.

"Hang on tight, Diane!" she stammered as she realized they were in trouble.

Diane, still on Louise's back, didn't have to be told. The dog had circled to the other side. A cow stampeded from the herd in a wild frenzy and knocked Louise down. Diane went tumbling to the ground.

Louise rose to her knees only to find herself looking face-to-face into a wall of snorting, wild-eyed beasts that were charging toward her like buffalo on a stampede.

With only a second to act, Louise fell down on top of Diane and tried to cover the little body with her own. She had time only to utter a prayer: "Jesus, help us! Save us!"

The thunder of hooves filled Louise's ears. Dust blinded her eyes and made her cough. She felt the ground rumble and quiver under her, and she tensed her body for the onslaught of the sharp, hammering hooves. Sharp hooves, hard hooves—pounding, driving, cutting, breaking!

But no hooves touched her.

Suddenly, the thundering stopped.

Diane was sobbing and trying to squirm out from underneath her big sister. Louise lifted her head and looked around slowly. The cattle were grazing again. On all sides of the girls, fresh hoof tracks told the story. There were hoof marks just inches away from where the girls' heads had been. And one of Louise's shoes was missing, apparently knocked off by a hoof.

Louise got up and lifted her sister. She brushed the dust off their clothes. "Diane, . . . are . . . are you all right?"

"Uh-huh. What happened?" Diane gazed curiously around.

Louise looked her sister over, then herself. Neither was hurt.

"They ran right over the top of us," Louise said, shaking her head in awe. "But an angel must have been over us because we didn't get hit once. Jesus protected us."

The two girls started walking across the pasture toward home. Teddy was behind them again.

"Where's your shoe?" Diane looked at Louise's feet.

"I couldn't find it," Louise answered. But she wasn't thinking very much about the shoe now. Other shoes could be bought easily enough. Another Diane couldn't be bought anywhere. Nor another Louise, for that matter.

12

Don't You Ever Try It!

by Murl Vance

When I was twelve years old, my family decided to go hunting for honey. Someone had read that you can find a bee tree by watching the direction in which bees fly after they become loaded with honey.

"I'll give a dollar to anyone who finds a tree with bees in it!" Dad announced.

Happy with the thought of having a winter's supply of honey just for the job of gathering it, we declared a family holiday. All of us—each going our separate way—set out to see who could find a hollow tree with honey stored inside.

After several hours of fruitless search—the bees just did not cooperate—I found myself down near the Colorado River, which ran a few miles from our home. Directly across the river from me stood a group of large trees that I was sure should have a colony of bees in them.

The big problem was that the nearest bridge over which I could cross the river was three or four miles upstream. To investigate those trees would take at least a six-mile walk just to reach them, and after that, there would still be the long walk home.

It was now midafternoon, and I could see that it would be dark before I got home if I went to the trees. It didn't take me long to decide that the hour was too late and the distance too far.

Then I had my brilliant idea. Why not just swim across? I had learned to swim a short time before this and could dog-paddle for perhaps a hundred feet before tiring out. From where I was standing, I could see that the river had an island in it, and the width of the river between me and the island was not very great. I decided to swim over to the island and see what the stream on the other side looked like.

I had often heard that the Colorado is a treacherous river and that many swimmers have drowned in it. My folks had warned us children of its dangers, but they had never actually told us not to swim in it. (They had never told us not to jump off a cliff either!)

I had a "safe" plan. There were some two-by-fours lying along the bank, and I would take one along to use as a float while I paddled toward the island with one hand. I sat down on the bank and removed my shoes and socks, tying them to the suspenders on my back. I rolled my overalls well up over my knees and waded in. The swim to the island was easy, and all was well—so far.

I walked across the island and looked at the river on the other side. The water looked swifter and rougher and a little wider than the stream I had crossed. But there was another island between me and the distant shore, and I was sure that with my faithful piece of wood I would have no trouble. I waded out.

Disaster struck. Quicker than a flash, the swift current

snatched my wood from my hand. At about the same instant, the river took my feet out from under me. If I'd had any sense at all, I would have turned back to the island I had just left instead of heading for the opposite shore.

But I headed out. Immediately, I found myself in very real danger. I seemed to be going downstream at express speed, and time after time in the rough water, my head went under. Coughing and sputtering, I fought for my life. I greatly feared that I would be swept past the island and down to the main stream beyond.

I should have known that the rough water indicated rocks beneath the surface, but I never thought of them, though rocks have killed many swimmers in swift currents. Providentially, the water was deep enough so that I was not dashed against any of them in my desperate effort to reach the island.

I remember thinking, *My parents will never know what happened to me*, and several times I thought my last day on Earth had come. If I had been carried down past the end of the island, there's no question about what would have happened.

But my guardian angel was on the job. I reached the shore a short distance from the lower tip of the island. For a long time, I lay on the bank, coughing, too exhausted to stand up. Finally, I crossed over to the other side, and— horror of horrors—the stream was about twice as wide and apparently as swift as the one I had just crossed! I was marooned and didn't know which way to go.

Several times I crossed and recrossed the island, looking at the two streams. I knew good and well that I never wanted to get into the one I had just gotten out of, but the other one looked still worse! Desperately, I prayed for God to help me decide.

Finally, the fear of the known danger behind me proved more powerful than the fear of the unknown danger ahead. I decided to try the last stream, using another piece of wood I found. This time I was determined to hang on to that wood no matter what happened. Slowly and carefully, I waded out, almost pressing holes into the wood with my fingers.

To my amazement, the water was only about waist deep and not nearly so swift as it looked. Without difficulty, I waded across, not having to swim at all!

Sitting down on the far bank, I put on my wet socks and shoes and rolled down my trouser legs. By this time, I had long since lost interest in bee trees. I walked my weary way homeward, including those three miles to the bridge, thankful just to be alive and perfectly willing to let all the bees in the world keep their honey.

My experience taught me three valuable lessons: Don't ever, ever, ever swim in a river if you are not acquainted with the current. Don't ever go swimming by yourself. And don't think that a twelve-year-old boy knows more than his parents do about what is dangerous and what isn't!

13

Poison in the Loaves

by Helen Godfrey Pyke

osita laughed to herself as she swung the large mixing bowl at her side; her steps long and rapid. Blue-green mountains around the mission were like jewels sparkling in the Mexican sun. It was a beautiful Friday morning with the earth still damp from the morning shower, and it seemed that every bird in all Chiapas must be singing.

Hearing the birds made Rosita think of the musical program that would take place in the casa grande (big house) that evening. She and her friend Lupe would sing the new song they had learned.

The music teacher had praised them when she heard them practicing yesterday, and Rosita thrilled. Maybe someday, she thought, she could go to a village like the one she herself came from and teach the beautiful Christian music to other young people.

"Ho! Rosita!" Manuel's voice interrupted her thought.

"Buenas días, Manuel," she answered. ("Good morning, Manuel")

The kitchen boy shifted his load of fresh corn. "Our garden is growing so well. The cook is pleased to have many fresh vegetables to prepare for our table," he said proudly.

"You have been a faithful worker, Manuel," Rosita said with a smile.

She sensed Manuel wanted to rest and visit a few moments. "I'm sorry," she said reluctantly, "but I must hurry to get flour from the barrel in the storeroom. We have a big baking job to do before the Sabbath."

Manuel waved and headed for the mission kitchen. Rosita opened the storeroom door and peered inside. Yes, there was the barrel in the corner. She opened the lid and reached inside, but the scoop wasn't there. Her fingers explored inside the dusty barrel again. She looked around her. She didn't want to make a trip all the way back to the kitchen for another scoop on such a busy day. Maybe she could find something.

Outside on the table beside the door, she saw a large empty can. It was dusty. *That looks like flour on it*, she thought. *Maybe Manuel forgot it out here when he got flour yesterday.*

It didn't look dirty. Anyway, any germs that might be on it would be killed when they baked the bread. She would use it for a scoop. Rosita filled her bowl as full as she could carry it.

The rest of the day Rosita was terribly busy. She helped the cook sort beans, and then she mixed the bread. Later, she shaped it into loaves and baked them in the slow ovens. There were vegetables to prepare and fruit to wash for the meals on Sabbath. And the kitchen floor needed a real scrubbing. Rosita worked on it until the red tiles were spotless.

She had no time to think about the musical program.

She hardly had time to think about her school lessons.

Finally, it was suppertime, just a little before the beginning of Sabbath. Rosita sighed with relief, thinking how soon her work would be finished. Then she could relax and enjoy the quiet time and the singing.

She set the food on the tables and found a place for herself to eat in the kitchen. *The bread is still a bit warm,* she thought. *I won't eat any tonight.*

She smiled, thinking of the way the young men of the school always dug in when they had new whole-wheat bread. "I guess it seems like a real luxury after eating nothing but bread made from cornmeal or tortillas," she mused. She had worked so long in the kitchen that wheat bread was nothing new to her.

Twice during the meal, one table of boys came for more bread. Rosita chuckled to herself as she cut more slices and stacked them in fragrant piles.

"You are a good baker," Ramón said with a grin.

"I just helped the cook," Rosita said modestly.

Ramón smiled again. "But someday you will bake all alone. You are learning every day at your work."

Something about the way he said it made Rosita's cheeks burn. She liked Ramón very much. He was always so courteous and friendly. She wondered what he was thinking. She felt her heart fluttering as she tried to guess, for Ramón was already the assistant to the principal. There was talk that he might be sent out to teach a church school next year. He would not want to go alone.

She watched Ramón walk back to his table and begin eating another slice of her bread with his beans.

When the meal was finished, the kitchen workers rushed to clear the food away and wash the dishes. Rosita ran to the casa grande and met Lupe. They hummed through their duet together, then found two seats on the front row near the piano. The chapel room was filling rapidly. The music teacher started playing the organ, and someone else pulled the marimba into place.

Suddenly, a boy dashed into the room. "Is the doctor here?" he asked as he gasped for breath.

Rosita turned to watch the doctor leave. She tried to get her mind back on the singing, but she wondered who might be sick. It must be serious the way the boy from the clinic had been running. She opened her songbook and again read through the words to their duet.

Someone tapped her shoulder. Rosita looked up. The principal motioned for her to follow her outside.

As soon as they reached the front walk, the woman asked in an urgent voice, "Rosita, what did the boys at Ramón's table eat for supper tonight that the other students did not eat?"

Rosita thought. "Why, nothing, señora. We served the same foods to everyone." She paused. "They did eat three plates of bread I baked today. Could too much fresh bread make them sick?"

"Not this sick." The principal sighed. "The doctor is sure they suffer from food poisoning. Five of the young men have vomited, and they seem much better off. But Ramón and Paulo, who is bookkeeper in the clinic, are very ill. If the doctor knew what poison is causing the trouble, he could treat them more effectively. Can you think what might have gotten into the bread? Is there any rat poison in the kitchen that could have fallen into the dough?"

"Oh no, señora!" Rosita exclaimed. "Cook will not allow rat poison in the building."

"Well, come with me," the woman directed. "Perhaps we can trace down the trouble. If we hurry, we might help the doctor save those young men's lives."

Rosita gasped. Being sick was one thing. Dying was a different matter. She had thought that certainly the doctor would know something that could cure any trouble. But what if Ramón or Paulo died? What if she had poisoned them?

Her heart pounded, drowning out the sounds around her. Mechanically, she went into the kitchen.

"Now, let's repeat step by step how you made the bread today," the principal said.

Rosita nodded; her hands trembling and numb. "I measured out the water with this measuring pan—here. And yeast from this can—here. Then I added oil and molasses from these jars—here." She choked back a sob. "Then flour from the big bowl."

"Where did you get the flour?" There was an edge to the older woman's voice.

"From the barrel in the storeroom," Rosita answered.

"Was the barrel covered?"

"Oh yes, señora!" Rosita bit her lip. "But the scoop was missing. I used a can Manuel must have left on the porch."

Immediately, the woman called Manuel.

"Yes," he said. "I left the can there when I finished working in the lower garden early this morning. I used it to carry insecticide dust."

"That's it!" The principal turned and ran to the clinic.

The doctor pumped out the stomachs of Ramón and Paulo. He gave all seven boys medications to counteract the effects of the poisons.

"There must have been lumps of insecticide in the loaf

these boys ate," he said sadly. "The fine particles clinging to the can would be spread out so far in the whole batch of bread that they should not harm a person."

Rosita sat on the clinic steps with tears flowing. She watched Manuel pace up and down the walk. He was miserable, too, she knew. From the casa grande, marimba music and singing floated softly on the evening air. *Soon*, she thought, *there will be preaching and prayer.* She slipped into the clinic and waited for the doctor to look up.

"Could we have all the students pray?" she asked.

The doctor nodded. "I have been praying myself for an hour, but it would be a good thing to have the others pray too."

Rosita went in by the side door and whispered to the pastor, who sat listening to the music. He rose and spoke to the group. Everyone was suddenly sober. Everyone liked the assistant principal and the clinic's bookkeeper. In the hushed room, the students banded in small companies to pray. Rosita listened to the earnest voices around her. If God would only give them their request!

With a heavy heart, Rosita went to bed late that night. The principal said she could do nothing to help, so she should stay in her room. Why hadn't she smelled the insecticide? It was all her fault!

Soon after midnight, the woman roused the girls. "The two boys are much worse," she said as they gathered in the hall. "The doctor says their fevers are dangerously high and asks us to spend an hour praying."

On her knees, Rosita felt hope ease into her heart for a few moments. But when the others had returned to their beds, she still knelt by her window, pleading with God to repair the damage she had done.

In the morning, the doctor announced that he despaired of the two lives. The poison had worked so long. Their fevers still raged, and their pulses were erratic. He suggested that everyone at the mission should fast and pray that God would save them.

The day went by like a horrible dream for Rosita. She knew her faith should be stronger. Still, she kept thinking it might be presumptuous to expect God to intervene when she had been careless. Could He forgive her?

Whenever a door opened, she dreaded seeing a messenger from the clinic saying that the end had come for one of the boys.

Late in the afternoon, the doctor stepped into the casa grande. His face relaxed for the first time that day.

"I believe God has given us our request," he said. "Both Paulo and Ramón are resting quietly now. Their fevers are down, and their hearts are beating normally. In a few hours, they should be much better. Let us give thanks!"

Rosita slipped out of the chapel and looked across the mission grounds to the clinic. The sun was low over the mountains to the west, casting a golden glow, like a promise, over the school.

"Thank You, Father in heaven," she whispered. She knew He had forgiven her carelessness. The burden lifted now. Her prayers were answered. From inside came the sound of the organ. The other students burst into a hymn of praise. Rosita's own heart joined in the song: "Más allá del sol, / más allá del sol, / yo tengo un hogar." ("Beyond the sun, I have a home")

14

Broken Axle

by Margery Wilson

ometimes I wonder if we don't pray too much."
Bob held the back door for his father, who stopped to snatch
up two milk pails.

"Whatever made you say that, son? I thought you
enjoyed worship."

"Oh, it's OK. It's just that praying the same prayer day
after day kind of rubs." Bob shoved his hands deep in his
overalls. "Dad, if you had a dollar for every time you asked
God to protect and care for us, you'd be a rich man. Right?"

The older man studied his sturdy teenage son for a
moment before he replied. "I don't know. I just never
thought of it in that light. I guess it would bring in more
than a thousand dollars a year, figuring prayer three times
a day." Father grinned at Bob. "Who's going to pay this?"

"Oh, no one." Bob shrugged. "But what I couldn't do
with a thousand dollars! No school bill to worry about."

"Son, your life is worth a lot more than that. At least, to
me." Father leaned against the machinery shed. "We don't

always know when God protects us. Sometimes you feel death's brush, and suddenly, you know it's only a miracle you're alive. God has intervened, or you wouldn't be here."

Bob forgot this serious conversation with his father in the busy weeks that followed. He spent most of his time plowing with the old McCormick-Deering 15-30 tractor.

He didn't even remember the conversation the morning his tractor clunked to a halt and tipped to one side. One of the huge wheels fell flat to the ground.

"Look at that! A broken axle right in the middle of plowing time. Of all the luck!" he muttered.

Even with Father to help and plank for leverage, it took a lot of puffing to load the five-foot steel wheel onto the truck bed.

"I'm afraid we can't weld it. This axle has crystallized near the break. It would only break again," Bob observed.

"Well, let's just take this piece of axle out of the wheel and see if we can find a used one to fit the hub. I'll bet Zeke's junkyard has an old four-inch axle," Father suggested.

He and Bob pulled and pushed at the broken piece of axle for an hour, using every tool in the shed. Finally, Father wearied. "We're wasting our time. This is a job for Uncle Nim."

Uncle Nim ran the blacksmith shop in town. Everyone called him Uncle Nim, and almost everyone had occasion to call on him for help to keep old farm machinery running in those Depression days.

Uncle Nim knew a hard job when he saw one, but he liked to tease. "Why don't ye jes' go an' buy ye one of them fancy new rubber-tired wheels fer that tractor," he said with a grin.

"Then I'd have to buy another one for the other side of the tractor." Father laughed.

Uncle Nim knew that Father didn't have money for rubber tires. He grew serious. "We'll have to pound it out. It'll take a bit more force. Quite a bit."

Uncle Nim directed them to mount the wheel on a special stand, blocking it up from the floor. Then he rammed a driveshaft into the open end of the hub.

"This here's a special gadget fer stubborn stickin' jobs. Jes' a piece of pipe welded to a piece of shaft. Here, hold this handle steady, son."

Bob grabbed the pipe handle while the blacksmith swung a sledgehammer down onto the end of the shaft. The wheel wiggled, but nothing fell out below.

"Must be hung up on a little rust. We'll have to heat it up," Uncle Nim declared.

"What good will that do? They're both steel." Bob leaned down to squint at the broken piece.

"Naw. That hub is cast iron. Iron don't expand much, and that axle can't expand up against the cast iron. It will have to expand lengthwise when it gets hot."

The blacksmith saw that Bob still looked puzzled. "We'll cool the hub, which will shrink it, but the steel axle will still be hot and expanding lengthwise."

"That might give a few thousandths of an inch clearance to jar the old thing loose," Father said with an air of "let's get going," and they did.

Sweat sparkled on their faces as the men heated the tractor wheel to a red-hot heat with weed-burner torches. A fine spray of cold water on the red-hot wheel created steam to add to their discomfort and the tension of the task.

Then Father stepped onto the small platform, and his sledgehammer rang hard against the driveshaft but with no results.

Uncle Nim watched for several minutes. The heat of the atmosphere and the unyielding task fomented a stormy steam within his mind.

"Here, let me at that." The huge, muscular blacksmith grabbed the sledgehammer. "I'll put my two hundred twenty-five pounds on the end of that maul."

In obvious anger, he swung the sledgehammer in a complete circle, pulling down on its three-foot handle with all his strength. The head of the hammer landed again and again on the driveshaft sticking in the wheel hub.

Bob stood directly across the wheel from Uncle Nim, holding the handle of the driver steady and feeling glad that it extended four feet from the shaft that was receiving the tremendous blows.

Although the boy never once diverted his attention from his task, he absorbed an awareness of Uncle Nim's tremendous physical strength. Muscles rippled, unhindered by an ounce of fat. No wonder they called him Nimrod. The name seemed to fit this six-foot-two giant who could swing a maul as if it were a matchstick and fling an un-Christian vocabulary even further—horrifying prim church ladies and fascinating young boys of the small town. Bob smiled in the heat, remembering how his mother had washed his mouth with soap the first time he repeated some of the words he had heard in the blacksmith's shop.

Suddenly, Bob felt he should change his position a quarter of a turn around the hub and stand to one side instead of directly across from the flushed, infuriated blacksmith. It would be harder to hold the handle in that position, Bob argued with himself, but the impression persisted. The teenager stepped around the wheel two short steps, clenching the pipe handle with a firmer grip.

At that exact instant, the heavy maul head left the handle in midair and slashed through the air directly toward the spot that Bob had just vacated. It landed on the dirt floor with a tremendous thud.

Father yelled, and Uncle Nim stood stone silent; his flushed face turning white. A trembling hand dropped the sledgehammer handle.

"Bob, me boy, why did ye move? That maul would hev splattered yer brains if ye had stayed there. Whyever did ye move?" Uncle Nim slumped down to sit on the platform to ponder and weep in thankfulness.

"I don't know, Uncle Nim." Bob tried to control the quiver in his own voice. "You won't ever believe me, but I think it was God."

Uncle Nim shook his head in wonder and stared at the two separated pieces of sledgehammer and at Bob.

An hour later, Bob and his father loaded the tractor wheel onto the old truck bed and placed the broken piece of axle beside it. Father slid behind the wheel to drive. Then he smiled at Bob. "Do you still think we pray too much?"

"Nope!" Bob knew death had brushed too close for comfort, and he couldn't find any other word just then.

His father answered for him. "God put on a real show of His power today. He saved my son's life and shook up an old blacksmith who thought God was just an adjective. Bet that's the first sermon he ever saw."

Bob nodded in agreement. "I don't think he'll forget it. I know I won't!"

15

"Run Along and Play With the Bear"

by Douglas Cooper

Marilyn VanderMeer was busy ironing in the cozy living room of their log house. With her nearest neighbor twenty miles away and the closest town more than two hundred miles down the road to the south, it seemed there would be plenty of time to just relax and enjoy wilderness living. But the VanderMeers' life was a very busy one.

They operated a lodge and service station on a remote stretch of the Alaska Highway. Deep in the heart of Canada's intriguing Yukon Territory, their lonely little outpost provided a stopping place for motorists and truckers on the long and sometimes difficult journey from the States to Alaska.

Sid VanderMeer could be proud of the way he ran his business. He was known up and down the highway as someone who could be counted on to help those in trouble. Often he was called out with his tools or his wrecker truck to assist some motorist in distress.

This would leave his wife, Marilyn, to take care of things

while he was gone. She was used to having her cooking or her ironing interrupted by someone needing gas for their car or even some help with changing a tire. Summer was the busiest time of all with the many tourists on the road.

This particular day was even more hectic than usual. Sid had been called up the road to work on a stalled car. Marilyn was trying especially hard to get her ironing finished before another interruption came.

Their two-year-old daughter, Rosa, was contentedly playing by herself in the kitchen. Marilyn was glad the little girl was staying out of the way for the moment so she could get the work done.

Suddenly, Rosa came around the corner into the living room. She toddled across the floor as fast as her chubby legs would carry her and began to pull at her mother's dress.

"Mommy, Mommy, there's a bear in the kitchen," she said matter-of-factly.

Mrs. VanderMeer, wondering when her husband would be home and what she should fix for supper, did not really hear what Rosa said.

"Run back and play some more now, honey," she replied. "Mommy will be through here before long."

"But Mommy," the tyke persisted, pulling all the harder on the dress, "there is a bear in the kitchen."

This time Marilyn understood what her daughter was saying. She smiled inwardly to herself. Yesterday there had been a lion under the porch. The day before that there had been a baby elephant in the bathtub. It seemed that her little girl had a typical two-year-old's imagination.

Rosa released her grip on her mother's dress and skipped back toward the kitchen, evidently giving up any hope of getting her attention.

Marilyn went on with her ironing. But Rosa was soon back beside her. This time she really tugged at the hem of her mother's dress.

"Mommy," she said, "please come and see the bear in the kitchen."

"Rosa," Marilyn said, a little bit exasperated now, "I am busy, so you will just have to leave me alone for a little while longer. Why don't you run along and play with the bear until I am through? Maybe we can invite him to stay to supper with us."

Rosa looked up at her mother for a long moment. "All right, Mommy," she said as she turned and left the room.

Just then, something fell to the floor with a terrific crash out in the kitchen.

Marilyn turned from her ironing board and said, "Rosa, what are you . . ." But she never finished the sentence. Rosa had not reached the kitchen. She was just rounding the corner.

"Rosa!" Mother screamed. "Come back here!"

Knocking over the ironing board and the iron in her haste, Marilyn raced toward her daughter and scooped her up in her arms. Quickly, she ran toward the bedroom and slammed the door shut behind them.

"Rosa," she said, "there really is a bear in the kitchen, isn't there?"

"Yes, Mommy," the little girl replied. "I told you there was, Mommy."

They heard another crashing sound as Marilyn put Rosa on the bed. What was she to do? Her husband might not be home for some time yet. There was no one else around for miles to help. The bear could easily crash through the bedroom door.

There was only one thing to do. As the rattling and banging noise continued to come from the kitchen, Marilyn reached for a rifle that hung on the log wall. With trembling fingers, she slipped a cartridge into its chamber as she had seen her husband do.

"Rosa," she said, trying to conceal the fear in her voice, "you stay right here and don't leave the bedroom."

Taking a deep breath, Marilyn opened the door slightly and stepped out, shutting it securely behind her.

The sounds from the kitchen ceased. The animal must have heard her.

Raising the rifle to her shoulder, the young mother moved cautiously toward the corner wall that separated the two rooms. She stepped into a position where she could look into the kitchen, and there it was—a huge black bear!

The rifle went off with a tremendous roar. The bear twisted and clawed the air and attempted to move forward. Marilyn desperately tried to get another shell into the chamber of the gun. She struggled with the bolt and pulled the trigger, but nothing happened! The rifle was jammed. She had failed to load it properly.

But that second bullet was unnecessary. The powerful five hundred-pound animal lay where it had fallen. Now she saw that it had entered the kitchen through an unlatched window.

Breathing a prayer of thanks for their safety, Marilyn went back to the bedroom and took her frightened little girl in her arms.

"Rosa," she said, "next time you try to tell me something, I'm going to listen."

16

A Bear Hitchhiker?

by Cora Mae Thomas as told to Inez Storie Carr

Where we should take our vacation had been a topic of discussion for weeks at our house.

"I think it would be nice to get away from this ninety-degree weather for a while," said my husband. He was a medical doctor in Keene, Texas. "Let's go to Yellowstone National Park."

So we headed to Wyoming. For the four days we spent at West Thumb Village in Yellowstone, we forgot it was summer. In fact, David, our nine-year-old son, came running one morning with a piece of ice from the grass. The thermometer stood at twenty-two degrees.

For four days, we matched our inexperienced wits with the experienced wits of bears. Little bears, big bears; brown bears, black bears; mama, papa, and children bears all wanted a handout.

"Go away; go away!" I shouted at the tourist-fed fat bear tummy that stretched up and beyond the window of our car. The claws and head that went with the tummy were investigating our cartop pantry. But these bears were not the go-away kind.

Their bored-looking faces seemed to say, "How stingy can a tourist be?"

"I've had enough of this sleeping with bears. Let's move on," stated my husband on the fourth day after having the car tipped, jolted, and shaken by our friendly four-legged neighbors every night.

We drove fifty miles down the West Road along the bank of the river toward Madison Junction. A full orange moon jeweled Old Faithful's two hundred–foot irregular spoutings and spread a golden veil over the winding river.

Suddenly, the car began to rock and roll like a ship in an ocean storm.

"There must be a big bear on top of the car!" shouted David from the backseat as he snatched at the rear of the front seat to steady himself.

We drove faster and faster over the bumpy, twisting trail.

"That ought to shake him loose," laughed Linda.

But the swaying and rocking of the car continued. When we reached Madison Junction and I saw people grouped by the road, I frantically called even before we reached them, "Is there a bear on top of our car?"

"No, there's an earthquake!" came the almost-as-frantic answer from several in unison.

Then a ranger stepped to the driver's window and asked in awe, "Where did you come from?"

"Over the Madison trail," my husband replied.

"That road is closed. An earthquake just slid a mountain over it. How did you get through?"

"So it wasn't a bear!" I gasped.

"No," said the ranger. "You missed death by minutes. Earth tremors, not a bear hitchhiker, was giving your car the rock-and-roll treatment."

Just then, the earth again shuddered and heaved. We didn't know what the next moment might bring, but it seemed the worst was over. My husband counted more than forty-two tremors.

We had made the fifty-mile trip between two big earthquake shakes that had tumbled boulders up to two tons' weight down on the road, smothered it with depths of mountain soil, and broken open great fissures or chasms in the road we had just passed over.

Whom do you think we thanked for the fact that we were not under the mountain?

17

Snowbound!

by Virginia H. Maas

Dan leaned back in his chair and stretched out his long legs as he eyed his two friends Bob and Larry. "I think we could make it. We've climbed other mountains without any trouble. Smaller ones, of course, but—"

"But this is late autumn, and Mount Hood is over eleven thousand feet high," Bob said doubtfully. He was fifteen and a year younger than his two companions. "What do you think, Larry?"

"I'm all for it." Larry's optimism was contagious, and soon even Bob joined in the excited planning.

"When should we make the climb?" Dan asked. "Let's set a date now."

"How about the fifteenth?" Larry suggested.

"Sounds great as far as I'm concerned." Dan ran his hands through the dark hair that fell over his forehead. "The next step will be to get our parents to OK the idea. I think my folks will agree to it. What about you two? Do you think you can get permission?"

Bob hesitated, but Larry nodded quickly. "No problem. They've never objected before to my mountaineering."

Bob's stubby fingers rubbed his freckled nose. "I think my mom and dad will agree as long as you both are allowed to do it."

"Then it's settled," Dan said. "That will give us plenty of time to prepare very carefully."

For the next two weeks, the three boys spent much time together, talking, planning, and collecting provisions for their ascent of spectacular Mount Hood. The morning of the fifteenth they waved goodbye to their parents and began their attempt at the summit.

The weather was slightly overcast but not enough to worry the boys as they climbed.

"We're really getting up there," Dan said as they paused for a short rest on the beautiful cone-shaped mountain. "We've kept up a pretty good pace."

"We sure have." Bob was panting as he leaned against a huge rock. "The rest of the way will be harder, won't it?"

Larry nodded his blond head. "Don't worry. You'll make it."

By nightfall, all three were ready to find a sheltered spot, eat some beans, and bed down for the night.

The next morning Dan roused his two companions early. "We'd better get back on the trail quick," he said.

"The weather doesn't look too promising." Larry frowned slightly as he crawled from his sleeping bag and peered at the sky.

"That's why we should get going as soon as we can," Dan admitted.

By late afternoon, snow was falling heavily. At the nine thousand-foot level, the boys were moving at a snail's pace in the midst of a howling blizzard.

"I can't see where I'm going!" Bob complained with fear in his voice.

The swirling snow beat against them, blinding their eyes and numbing their feet and hands.

"We can hope the storm will let up," Larry yelled in order to be heard above the whistle of the wind as they huddled against a rock wall. Even as he spoke, he realized the storm was not abating. In fact, it was worsening.

Dan sized up the situation. "We'll have to dig ourselves a snow cave."

They dug furiously into the huge snow mounds as the temperature around them plunged rapidly.

"Feels like at least thirty below zero," Dan shouted to Larry, who was next to him.

Inside the homemade cave, they crouched close to one another to share whatever body heat was generated.

Dan felt a great wave of guilt invading his thoughts. It had been his idea to climb Mount Hood, and now his friends were endangered and miserable. He shouldn't have suggested it so late in the year.

"I could kick myself for getting you two into this," he said. "I didn't—"

"It's not your fault," Larry assured him. "I wanted to do it as much as you did, so don't blame yourself."

"We should be able to dig out in the morning and start back down before another storm hits." Dan tried to inject a tone of confidence into his voice for Bob's sake. He knew the younger boy was sick with fear.

Suddenly, a feeling of strength and hope brought tears to Dan's eyes. "I know our folks at home are thinking of us and praying for our safety. Imagine them in your minds, both of you, and I think you'll feel more peaceful inside, like I do."

Taking Dan's advice, the other boys lapsed into silence.

Then Larry said, "Let's sing some hymns, like 'A Mighty Fortress,' to encourage ourselves."

"Hey, that's a good idea," said Bob, feeling less panicked about their predicament.

Later, before they settled into their double-thickness sleeping bags for some rest, the three joined hands while Dan prayed for protection and a safe return to their homes.

In the morning, they ate some of their dehydrated food after melting snow under their shirts to have drinking water.

"Now that we've eaten, we'd better try to tunnel out." Dan turned to his companions uneasily. He wondered how much snow blocked the cave entrance.

The three worked feverishly as they realized the depth of their cold, white shelter. Again Dan's feeling of guilt nearly overwhelmed him. He knew that no one had ever before survived in a snow cave on Mount Hood for more than five days. Would they be trapped for good and die from lack of air?

No, surely God wouldn't leave them here. They'd do their part by digging and let God do the rest.

"I'm getting winded," Bob complained as he gasped for air.

"Don't talk," Larry said. "Save your breath. Just dig."

Wearily, they kept at it. After they had dug away what Dan guessed was forty feet of snow, they pierced through to the outside world and fresh air.

"I thought we'd never make it," Larry said later as they breathed deeply of the cold but welcome air.

The snow had let up a bit, but the wind continued to

hurl it savagely at the mountainside. "We aren't out of trouble yet," Dan sighed. "We'll have to dig another cave and kind of hibernate for a while. The visibility is still too poor to start a descent."

"Let's rest before we start on a new cave," Bob said. "I haven't recovered from digging out of the old one yet."

"Yeah," Larry agreed vigorously.

After alternating digging and resting periods, the boys were huddled together in a new snow cave.

"If it weren't for our thick wool clothes and these down parkas, we'd have frozen to death for sure." Larry patted his jacket appreciatively.

Bob grimaced. "Don't even talk about dying. We came too close for comfort this time."

"Let's read from the Bible awhile." Dan took out his pocket copy and began to turn the pages. "Any special place?"

"I like the psalms," Larry answered. "But anywhere is good."

After reading for some time, Dan began to tell stories, including some of the funny experiences he'd had when he was younger. Then he entertained his two companions with impersonations—a talent he had recently acquired.

His audience laughed heartily. "Feels good to have fun again, even if we are freezing." Larry snuggled further into his sleeping bag. "Tell us some bedtime stories, Daddy," he added, imitating the high voice of a small child as he looked over at Dan.

Dan snorted, then began to relate the stories he remembered from a Mother Goose book he'd received for his fourth birthday. He knew it would sound odd to his friends in Portland if they ever found out the boys had resorted to nursery rhymes, but he also knew how important it was to keep a sense of humor when facing this kind of situation.

They needed this optimism as the days went by, finally adding up to two weeks. During this time, the boys became weaker, but they continued to pray. Whenever threatened by cave-ins and avalanches, they burrowed into new caves.

"This is the last cave I ever want to dig," Bob complained breathlessly as they finished the eighth one. "I don't think I can do another one."

"Cheer up. This may be the last one we'll have to dig," Dan said. "After sixteen days of blizzards, the weather is bound to change." He tried to sound more optimistic than he felt.

The next morning the trapped boys shouted for joy when they saw a bright-blue sky.

"The storm is over!" Larry shouted, clapping Dan on the back. "We're going to get down alive!"

Two hours later, Dan couldn't believe his eyes when he saw a snow tractor coming toward them. "They've found us!" he shouted.

A rescue helicopter soon arrived to fly the climbers to the base of the peak.

From that day, Mount Hood was more than just a beautiful mountain to the three boys. It had become a symbol of God's love and protection.

18

Thirteen Who Prayed

by Kay Warwick

The water's rising! What shall we do?" asked little Andy; his voice high and shrill with fear.

Everyone else in the room looked around anxiously at each other. Mrs. Smith hushed her young daughter, Susan, and Pastor Crouse got to his feet. His thin face was drawn with worry, but his blue eyes had a look of peace. "We'll go up to the second floor," he announced calmly. "Come on, everybody. Mrs. Smith, bring your little one."

The thirteen people who hurriedly climbed the stairs of an old frame house that night in Corpus Christi, Texas, were seeking refuge from a ferocious hurricane. With the exception of Pastor Crouse, they were women, old men, and children. The other men in the congregation were out helping to build a protective seawall out of sandbags.

The wind's terrible force battered the old wooden house, actually swaying it from time to time.

White-haired Mr. Broderick crept close to the minister during a lull in the storm's noise. "Elder Crouse, what are we going to do?" he asked. "The water's getting higher by the minute."

The pastor patted him gently on the shoulder. "Don't worry; there's an attic above this floor. That's where we'll go next. Remember, we mustn't panic. Instead, we must trust in God for deliverance." With that, he took a blanket and walked over to wrap it around a little girl.

Afterward, the pastor stayed close to a window, anxiously watching the level of the dark, turbulent waters. Occasionally, a tree trunk or part of another building would crash against the house, causing everyone to wince nervously.

When the water had almost reached the windowsill, Pastor Crouse made his decision. "All right, it's time to go up into the attic," he said firmly.

He helped the group clamber up a ladder, which was the only way to the attic. When everyone was settled, he said, "Friends, I think we should all kneel and pray to Him who is even now watching over us."

Everyone slipped to their knees, even the smallest child. As the minutes crept by, they took turns praying.

After the last prayer, Pastor Crouse started to speak. He was interrupted by the sounds of knocking close to the attic window. It was regular, rhythmic, steady.

"What's that?" one woman cried; her voice squeaking with fright.

"Don't be afraid," Pastor Crouse said softly, standing up. "I'll see what it is." He crossed to the window and leaned far out.

Moments later, he drew back inside with a hopeful expression and a rope in his hand.

"Our prayers have been answered!" he exclaimed. "An

empty boat was making the noise. It must've broken loose from its mooring. I'll hold the rope while you all climb aboard. Now we have a way to escape!"

The others rushed to the window, all trying to look out at once.

"But it's only a skiff," Mr. Broderick said in deep disappointment. "It's not nearly big enough for all of us."

"Now wait a minute," the minister declared. "God sent it to us, so I know it'll be large enough. Come on; we must load the boat while the wind's not blowing. It won't be long till the attic isn't safe any longer. Besides, the house may be torn from its foundation at any moment."

Somehow, all thirteen people crowded themselves into the tiny skiff. Using tree branches for oars, they managed to navigate the craft away from the dangerously teetering house.

During the night, the small band of survivors floated along and avoided being capsized by the waves and the menacing debris surrounding them. Their prayers sustained them, and in the morning, a larger boat picked them up and brought them to safety.

Grand Canyon Rescue

by Leslie L. Lee

G irls, the sun is coming up," Dad called, shaking the tent flap. "We have to get going if we're going to climb down into the Grand Canyon today."

"My back aches," moaned Jenni. "The ground isn't much of a mattress under these sleeping bags." She opened her eyes and squinted at the dim sunlight filtering through the tent screen.

"Time to wake up, Stef," she said. She reached over and shook her sister. Stephanie mumbled something and pulled her sleeping bag over her head.

With a little nudging, everyone was finally up and enjoying a good breakfast. "Here are some crackers and fruit bars," Dad said, handing them to the girls. "I'll carry the food for our overnight stay at the bottom of the canyon."

"Just don't eat the snacks now," Mom said with a smile.

Soon the hikers and their gear were piled into the van. Dad said a short prayer, asking God to bless their day and protect them as they enjoyed seeing His nature.

A short time later, the family pulled into the parking lot at the South Rim of the canyon. Shouldering their backpacks, the hikers headed toward the trail.

"Before we start out, let's look at the trail map," Dad wisely suggested. He unfolded the map and laid it on the stone ledge overlooking the canyon. "We may get separated on the trail, so let's plan on meeting at the first rest stop. It's about a mile down."

Adjusting their packs, the family set out. The trail was dusty and narrow, and often they had to move to one side to let oncoming hikers pass by.

"Ouch!" Jenni cried out as she slipped and sprawled backward onto the trail. Getting to her feet, she brushed the dirt off her jeans and picked gravel from the palms of her hands.

"Don't be in such a hurry," Stephanie counseled. "And remember, put your weight on the balls of your feet. That's what I read in a trail guide."

"Yes, 'Mother,' " Jenni responded with a twinkle in her eyes.

Just then, the girls heard a noise behind them. Looking back, they saw a mule train coming down the trail. They watched as the animals moved by with their riders perched high on their backs.

"Boy, I'm sure glad we didn't decide to ride them down this narrow, steep trail!" Stephanie exclaimed. "I wouldn't want to sit up there, even if mules are supposed to be sure-footed animals."

"One slip and look out below!" Jenni commented. "That's too scary even to think about."

"Let's stop and rest down there under one of those piñon trees," Mom suggested. She pointed at a group of scrubby trees a few feet ahead.

"Agreed," Dad responded. A few minutes later, the four hikers were sprawled out under the trees.

Suddenly, a small animal waddled across the trail. "What was that?" Jenni asked.

"That was a spotted skunk," Dad informed them. "They're quite common in Arizona."

After a few restful minutes, Dad rose to his feet. "Well, it's time to hit the trail again."

The hikers hoisted their backpacks up and set out on the next leg of their journey. As Dad had predicted, the family became separated. Jenni and Stephanie were the first to arrive at the rest area they'd designated as a meeting place. After a short rest and a drink of water, the girls gazed up the trail but didn't see their parents.

"Let's go on ahead," Stephanie suggested. "We'll see Mom and Dad at the bottom."

"Cool," Jenni replied. "Let's go."

After a tiring trek, the girls finally reached a mesa they had spotted from the rim of the canyon. "Am I glad to see level ground!" Stephanie breathed a sigh of relief.

"Now we should really make good time," Jenni asserted. "Let's not even stop at the rest area ahead."

The trail stretched out ahead as far as their eyes could see before disappearing in the distance. A half hour later, the girls came upon a fork in the trail.

"Do you remember seeing this spot from up above?" Stephanie asked her sister.

"Sure," Jenni replied. "A trail branched off to the left of the main trail and went toward the side of the canyon. It doesn't look like it's used much, though."

"Let's hike over there," Stephanie suggested. "I bet I can get some great photos of the Colorado River from that area."

The girls left the main trail and headed for the side of the canyon. The trail was deserted. There weren't even any shoe or boot tracks.

"Stephanie, I don't like this," Jenni said in a shaky voice as they walked along. "What if something happened to us? No one would even know it."

"Don't worry," Stephanie chided. "Nothing's going to happen to us. We'll just take a few photos. Then we'll go back to the main trail."

A few minutes later, the two sisters surveyed the beauty of the river far below. The sun glistened on the brown-and-yellow rocks lining the canyon.

"Awesome!" exclaimed Jenni. "I can hardly wait to get down to the bottom."

"Me too!" Stephanie said, climbing over the rocks at the edge of the trail. "Let's see now. If I can just get a little closer, I can get a shot of the rapids and—" Suddenly, Stephanie let out a shriek. *"Ohhh!"*

Jenni glanced over to see her sister topple over the trail's edge and her arms flailing in all directions. Stephanie's camera flew high in the air as she disappeared far below.

"Stephanie! Stephanie!" Jenni called, looking down in horror from the spot where she had last seen her sister. "Where are you? Are you all right?"

There was no response—only the sound of the soft breeze blowing through the trees below.

"Stephanie! Stephanie!" Jenni called frantically. But she heard no sound from her sister.

How far down is she? Is she still alive? The questions tumbled through Jenni's mind. *What do I do now?*

She knew the answer was prayer. Kneeling at the edge of the trail, Jenni poured out her heart to God. "Dear Jesus, please be with Stephanie. Help her not to be hurt too bad. And help me know what to do. I know You love us and are with us even in trouble. Amen."

"Stephanie!" Jenni called again, straining to peer over the edge. "Stephanie, I'm going for help."

Leaving her backpack on the side of the trail to mark the scene, Jenni ran for help. She screamed when she saw a pink rattlesnake slither across her path.

She spotted two hikers coming down the trail. "Do either of you have a cell phone?" she asked urgently. "My sister fell over the edge of the canyon!"

"Sure don't," one of the hikers responded. "But I saw a ranger at the rest station. I'm sure someone there can help you."

Jenni ran on. She was getting tired, but she had no choice but to keep running.

Oh, dear God, be with Stephanie until I can get help for her! she prayed silently.

Rounding a bend in the trail, Jenni ran smack into her father, almost knocking him to the ground. She began sobbing uncontrollably.

"Dad, . . . Stephanie . . . ," Jenni stammered as tears coursed down her cheeks.

"Calm down, honey," her father said, giving his daughter a comforting pat on the back. "Where's Stephanie? Has something happened to her?"

Mom soon joined them. "Don't ask so many questions," she urged her husband. "Give Jenni a chance to get her thoughts together."

Within a few moments, Jenni stopped crying and told the whole story of what had happened.

Dad looked back up the trail. "We just left the second

rest stop," he explained. "I remember seeing a ranger there. Let's hurry back and tell them what's happened."

Soon the threesome arrived at the ranger station and explained the situation. Immediately, a ranger was on a cell phone, relating the incident. He hung up and turned to the group.

"A chopper will be here in a few minutes." Then he told Jenni, "The pilot wants you to go with them to show the exact place you last saw your sister."

Hardly had the ranger stopped talking before the noise of a chopper could be heard in the distance. Soon it was on the ground, and a medic from the aircraft was running toward the building.

"Jenni, your mother and I are heading back to the rim," Father explained. "We'll see you at the lodge." They were out the door of the ranger station before Jenni could respond.

"Let's go find your sister," the medic commanded.

Jenni took her seat in the chopper next to the pilot. Two paramedics sat to her right. The helicopter climbed steadily and swung away from the building. Then it headed toward the canyon.

"I want you to point to the general area," the pilot shouted above the noise of the motor. "Then we'll go down and try to spot your sister."

"There's my backpack!" Jenni yelled, pointing to the red bag far below. "Stephanie fell just to the left of it."

The helicopter swooped down and moved over toward the crest of the canyon. Down, down the chopper crept. Jenni and the medics strained their eyes to catch a glimpse of the missing girl.

"There!" one of the men exclaimed, pointing. "A

boot—and just to the left is a red bandanna."

The helicopter quickly dropped and hovered over the spot. Farther to the left, a leg stuck out from under a bush.

"Oh no!" Jenni screamed. "Oh, dear God, help her to still be alive!"

The medics let down a rope ladder and a medical sled. Soon one of the men was on the ground. The chopper flew back to the rim, where the pilot set the aircraft down.

The other medic leaped out and pulled a rope from a winch. With the rope in both hands, he quickly went over the edge, heading down to meet his buddy.

Jenni was shivering, even though sunshine streamed through the windshield.

"It's going to be all right," the pilot said. "Before you know it, we'll have your sister to the hospital."

His words and her own prayers filled Jenni with an inner peace. She stopped shaking and began feeling the warmth of the sun.

Suddenly, the winch line jerked, indicating that the medics were ready for the sled to be pulled up. The pilot started the winch motor, which in turn began reeling in the line.

Jenni watched the line move ever so slowly. Then the sled appeared, followed by the two medics. They unhooked the line, transferred Stephanie to a stretcher, and hoisted it into the chopper.

Jenni glanced at Stephanie. A block on each side of her head held it stiff. Her face was black and blue. Red scratches stretched across her pale cheeks. Strands of hair, now matted with blood and dirt, streaked down her forehead. Her eyes were closed.

"We're going directly to the hospital in Flagstaff. That's

the closest medical facility," the pilot informed Jenni. "Your sister is in critical condition. We can't take the time to drop you off at the lodge. After we land and get her off, we'll take you back."

The town of Flagstaff soon came into view. When the chopper landed, two nurses raced out and whisked Stephanie inside the hospital. *Oh, God,* Jenni prayed silently, *be with Stephanie. Guide the emergency room medics, the doctors, and the nurses.*

After a few minutes, the pilot spoke. "Well, ready to head back?"

Jenni slowly nodded, and soon the chopper was headed toward the lodge. Her parents were waiting there when Jenni returned. They said another prayer before they got into the car to begin the two-hour road trip to the hospital. When they arrived, they learned that Stephanie had suffered a concussion, fractured a leg, broken an ankle and two ribs, and had internal injuries. But she was alive!

After three weeks in the hospital, Stephanie flew back home with her family. Even today they thank God for His goodness and mercy and for leading them to those who made the Grand Canyon rescue.

20

Out of Control

as told to Elisabeth A. Freeman

As I boarded the school bus, Mr. Whitmoore, the bus driver, glared at me. His cheeks looked red and puffy. *That's weird,* I thought. *He usually smiles and shakes my hand. Maybe he's just having a bad day.*

Brandy smiled and hollered, "Saved you a seat, Thomas."

"Thanks," I said. "Not too bad, either. Only six seats back."

"I tried to get closer," Brandy said with a frown, "but the little kids got here before I did." Since our bus picked up the grade-school kids first, teens from the middle school usually had to sit in the back.

I shrugged. "That's OK. This is great." I glanced out the window at the sun peeking through the clouds.

"Sure looks better than the rain we had this morning," Brandy said.

I nodded. She always chattered my head off. But today I didn't care. Nothing could ruin my plans. Soon I'd be home in my backyard, four-wheeling up and down the mountains.

As Mr. Whitmoore put his foot to the floor to climb the steep hill, the engine roared.

Everyone was doing their normal, everyday thing. Brandy rambled on as always. Bobby couldn't stop laughing after he poked Cindy with his pencil. When she turned around, he pretended Mark had told him a joke. Jimmy took a huge wad of gum and stuck it under the seat ahead of him. And Ryan hopped in and out of the empty seats like a rabbit, slowly making his way toward the front each time someone got off.

Setting my backpack down, I glanced at my watch and pulled out my math assignment. A half hour to go. That should give me plenty of time to get this done. As I worked on a tough problem, Mr. Whitmoore jerked the bus to a stop.

What's going on? Why are we stopping? I glanced up.

Mr. Whitmoore stood up, turned around, and glared at us with narrow, mean eyes. "Now I'm not gonna have you-all bein' rowdy!" Silence filled each seat. "If I have to stop this bus one more time, I'm gonna call the principal."

After he took his seat, everyone looked at each other and whispered.

I heard someone say, "What's his problem? We're not being any rowdier than we usually are."

Someone else said, "Yeah, why's he being such a pain?"

In the three months that Mr. Whitmoore had been driving our bus, I'd never seen him act like this. He always smiled, cracked jokes, and hummed a tune. I stared at him in his mirror. He didn't even look like himself. His whole face had turned completely red, and the bald spot on the back of his head was turning a bright pink.

He must really be having a bad day. I guess everyone has a bad day once in a while. Whatever it is, I'm going to keep to myself and get my work done.

A few minutes later, Brandy nudged me. "Look," she whispered, "he's grabbing our old write-up slips from under the seat."

When I glanced up, Mr. Whitmoore was leaning to the left with his arm dangling down. One of the boys muttered, "Why are we going to get in trouble for stuff we did a long time ago?"

Soon everyone started complaining. We heard Mr. Whitmoore radio in, but we couldn't make out what he was saying.

"Great! I didn't even do anything," I mumbled. Staring at my math book, I bit my lip and stayed still.

Ryan had worked his way up close to the front of the bus. *Good. It won't be much longer now.* When we came to Cindy's stop, Ryan opened the door for Mr. Whitmoore.

"Maybe he's sick," someone said as Ryan closed the door for him.

A strange feeling came over me as we continued up the huge hill toward Ryan's house. I heard the brakes and watched Ryan open the door and jump out. As the bus started moving down the big hill, my math book fell to the floor. After I scooped it up, I heard screaming and yelling. When I looked up, I realized the bus was out of control, going faster and faster down the mountain toward Mark's house.

Everyone ran to the back of the bus, but I raced to the front. Mr. Whitmoore was totally unconscious, hands on the wheel and foot on the gas. I peered out the windshield as we jumped the curb.

"God, please help me stop this bus!" I screamed as I

grabbed the steering wheel and reached my foot toward the brake.

But instead of slowing down, we sped even faster. Now the house was just five hundred feet away!

I tried to move Mr. Whitmoore's foot, but I couldn't. We hit the driveway with a huge bump that almost toppled the bus onto its side. I held on to the wheel as my body jiggled up, down, and from side to side.

The bouncy motion had knocked Mr. Whitmoore almost off the seat. The only thing I could see out of the windshield was Mark's house. I pressed again with my left foot, preparing to crash. The brakes screeched as we slid to a stop just inches from the porch.

While everyone exited out the back and others ran to get help, I realized we could have died. My hands shook, and my body quivered. I glanced at Mr. Whitmoore. He didn't seem to be breathing.

I hurried off the bus and sat on the curb as I waited for the ambulance. A few minutes later, sirens blared toward us. The paramedics put Mr. Whitmoore on a stretcher and loaded him into the back of the ambulance.

Soon afterward, a police officer approached me. "What happened here today?" he asked.

After I told him the whole story, he patted me on the back. "Nice job, son. You stopped the bus just in time."

"Yeah, you saved our lives," a lot of the other kids chorused as they slapped me high fives.

Although I felt relieved that the bus had stopped in time and that everyone except Mr. Whitmoore was all right, I knew God really deserved the credit for saving our lives. God heard my prayer and used my hands and feet to bring about the answer.

21

Stranded at Sea

by Eileen Bailey

Mother, this ship is so dirty," said Helen. "And the captain's wife walks funny."

"She's drunk," Mother said bluntly. "The ship is dirty because it carried coal from Belfast, Ireland, to Kingston. Although the captain promised to clean it up before we boarded, he doesn't seem to have taken his word seriously."

"We couldn't take a steamship back to the United States because your mother suffers so badly from seasickness," Father explained. "The motion on a steamship makes Mother's illness worse. We're just glad the captain of this little sailing vessel decided to take his wife to New Orleans for a visit and was willing to bring along some passengers."

The Steinhauers had been Moravian missionaries in Jamaica for several years. There Mother's consumption (tuberculosis) had improved, but Father's health had suddenly and completely failed. The doctors had advised him to return to the cooler climate of Pennsylvania. The family had hoped to take a more direct route home, but at least, they were leaving the heat of Kingston.

In spite of the poor conditions on the ship, Mother was sure they could bear it. "The voyage shouldn't take more than about a week," she reassured Helen.

"I hope so," Father said. "I heard a couple of the crewmen talking; there's enough food for only five days."

When the ship sailed the next morning, the captain had joined his wife in drinking the Jamaican rum they had taken aboard. Worse, being generous souls, they invited the sailors—even the cabin boy—to join them. The drinking spree lasted for days.

So they were not prepared when the storm hit. The drunken crew watched helplessly as the wind blew hour after hour, driving them far off course.

By the time the crew sobered up, the ship was becalmed, and they had no idea where they were. With no wind to stir the sails, the ship sat helpless in the sea.

Food and water quickly ran low. Everyone anxiously watched the horizon for signs of another ship.

Finally, "Ship ahoy!" A passing Yankee steamship had seen them! Passengers and crew rejoiced as a small boat put out from the steamship. The Yankee captain brought hard tack (ship's biscuits) and water. He also told the sailing vessel's captain the location of the ship.

But not long after the rescue ship steamed out of sight, another storm hit. When the storm finally ended, they were again lost.

Not a breath of air stirred to ease the heat of the Caribbean sun as it beat down on the little ship. Occasionally, Helen would put her hand on the wooden rail as she peered out to sea. Each time she snatched her hand back, burned.

At least Mother's seasickness disappeared while the ship

lay still. She wanted to come up on deck because the tiny, airless cabin was unbearably hot and reeked of her illness. But the sun was too hot. After a while, the kindhearted sailors thought of erecting an awning on the deck to shade the passengers.

Day after day, they watched. Occasionally, they would spot a ship in the distance, but always, it would sail on by without seeing them.

The days became weeks. The captain rationed everyone to half a ship's biscuit and one cup of water a day. The crew members lay listlessly about the deck, no longer singing or spinning yarns. Everyone prayed.

Helen was so hungry that she gnawed on one of her kid leather gloves, hoping to get some nutrition that way.

"Mother," she mumbled around her swollen tongue, "I'm so thirsty."

"We all are, dear," said Mother. It was torture to see water all around them and be unable to drink it. Mother wet some cloths with seawater and wrapped them around their throats. That helped. A little.

When nearly four weeks had passed, the captain made a chilling announcement. "We do not have enough food for everyone for tomorrow," he said sadly. "We will cast lots tonight. Tomorrow, just before the rations are passed out, you will be told the results. Then some of you will be thrown overboard. That way there will be one day's rations left for the rest."

Conscious of the sharks in the waters below, each person stepped up to draw a lot. They were all as skinny as skeletons. At last, the cabin boy stepped up. Since he had started the voyage fat, he had not wasted away as much as the others.

"Nay," said the captain, "not you."

At first, Helen thought the captain was being kind to the boy, but Father explained. "It's because the boy still has some meat on his bones," he said. "If a ship doesn't come soon, they'll eat the cabin boy."

Helen was horrified. "They wouldn't do that!"

"It's been known to happen at sea," said Father.

Father and the other male passenger decided to sleep on deck. Mother and Helen went below to the cabin.

"I'm going to pray all night," announced Mother. She knelt by her bunk and began to plead with God for rescue. Toward dawn, she fell asleep.

Suddenly, the door opened. Father came in and tapped Mother on the shoulder. "My dear, we think we see a sail," he said.

Mother was still groggy with exhaustion. Wearily, she remarked, "Oh, it will pass us by like all the rest."

Then she came fully awake. "God forgive me! It's an answer to my prayer!"

It was Father's turn to express doubt. "I would not have you disappointed," he said. "If it be God's will for us, the ship will come to our aid."

Weakly, Helen and Mother dressed and crawled up to the deck. Everyone was gathered at the rail, passing the spyglass back and forth. No one spoke.

Slowly, the black spot in the distance came closer and took on the distinct shape of a small steamship. Nobody on board the lost vessel had the strength to move or call out, even when the steamship hailed them. They just watched silently.

What the starving crew and passengers did not know was that the day before, the captain of this little steamship, who was an atheist (nonbeliever in God), had followed a very strange course of action.

The steamship was one of the towboats that helped sailing vessels into the harbor at New Orleans. Strict regulations limited the distance the towboats could go from port to look for ships needing help. But having reached the legal limit, this captain felt impelled to continue farther out to sea. His crew complained.

"You'll be fined for going beyond the limit."

"I know."

"Then why are we going on?"

"I don't know," replied the captain. "I just know I've got to go on! There's a ship out here somewhere."

Suddenly, the captain was stricken with seasickness. He had not been seasick for twenty years, but he was forced to take to his bunk. "Like a landlubber!" he complained.

Now the crew was sure he would turn back, but he still refused. Finally, they mutinied.

"We're almost out of food. We're not going a league farther!"

The captain bargained with them. "Please. Just till morning. If we don't see anything by then, I'll turn back."

Reluctantly, the crew agreed.

At dawn, the man at the masthead called out, "Object ahead! It's not movin', sir!"

"Make for it!" called the captain. "That's what we've come after." And just like that, his seasickness was gone.

Reaching the becalmed ship, the steamship crew put a boat in the water, and the captain and three other men crossed to the ship in which Helen and the others waited.

The towboat captain was the first to step on deck. When he saw the pitiful figures standing there, weak and skeletal, tongues swollen till their mouths would scarcely shut, he took off his hat.

"Now I believe," he intoned. "There is a God in heaven. And He has guided me to you."

Quickly, the men of the towboat shared what food they had. The big raw onion Helen received tasted so good that for the rest of her life, onions were one of her favorite foods.

Later, when the captain heard that Helen's mother had spent the night in prayer, he exclaimed, "Not only does God exist, but He surely hears and answers prayer."

22

Tsunami!

by Helena Welch

A lipati watched the stars through the open door of the hut and knew that morning was near. Today his father would put the baskets they had woven into the boat and take them around to the far side of the island to sell in the village.

Today I'll be alone! Alipati thought happily. *Today I can read the leaflets that Pastor Dionisio brought me. From them, I can learn more about Jesus.*

For several weeks, the pastor had been coming from the village and distributing literature among the island people. Alipati's father hadn't taken any literature, and he was angry when Alipati had done so. Once Alipati's father had torn up the leaflets. But there were some that Alipati had hidden under a stone behind the hut.

Soon a rooster crowed. Alipati left his bed to hurry outside. His father was already gathering up the baskets. "Help me load the boat," the man called. "I'll eat breakfast after I've started rowing."

"It will be a nice day for rowing," Alipati remarked eagerly.

"Yes," his father answered. "But we'll have bad weather soon. You'd better search Seaweed Cave for more firewood. Our supply is getting low."

Alipati's heart sank. When would he have time to read Pastor Dionisio's leaflets?

Seaweed Cave was far down the beach. There were always many pieces of driftwood left by the tide in and around the cave, but it would take most of the day to carry a few loads that long distance.

Sadly, Alipati stacked the last of the baskets in the boat and stepped back. His father took his seat and picked up the oars. "Mind, now. I want to see a big pile of wood when I return."

Alipati nodded. He watched until his father had rowed past a clump of trees, and then he turned back to the hut. After the boy had eaten breakfast, he stood undecided. Should he leave immediately for Seaweed Cave, or should he look at the literature?

At last, sighing, Alipati started for the cave.

I'll bring a load of wood first, he thought. *Then I can read for a few minutes. Surely Father won't care if I take a little rest.*

Alipati ran for a while along the sandy shore. Then he slowed down. He knew he must hurry so he would have more time for reading, but he didn't want to tire himself and not be able to carry the wood. At last, he reached the cave and collected his first load. Going home took more time, and his arms were very tired when he dumped the wood beside the hut.

Pausing only for a drink, Alipati hurried to the big

stone behind the hut and took out the leaflets. He brushed away the dirt and pieces of dried grass and began reading a portion from Psalms: "I will lift up mine eyes unto the hills, from whence cometh my help" (Psalm 121:1, KJV).

Alipati wasn't certain he knew what the words meant. He read them again. Then he looked up at the mountains behind the hut—a mass of bare, jagged rocks towering against the sky. They were the only hills the boy knew, but how could they ever help him?

For several minutes, he studied the mountains. Then something seemed to tell him to look in the opposite direction at the ocean. When he did, his mouth dropped open in surprise.

The ocean, instead of lapping inward as always toward the sandy beach, seemed to be crawling. Far, far out on the horizon, the water gathered in a gray wall that was growing higher and higher.

Suddenly, it dawned on Alipati what the wall meant. It was a huge wave that would soon come in and break onto the island. Never had Alipati seen such a wave, but he had heard of one that had come many years earlier. His grandfather had been washed away by it and never found again.

Alipati leaped to his feet; his mouth was dry with fear. He, too, might be washed away. Oh, what could he do? Trembling, he clasped his hands together and felt Pastor Dionisio's leaflet. The words he had just read flashed through his mind: "The hills, from whence cometh my help."

The answer struck him. The mountains! He could climb up into the mountains! Swiftly, he sped across the sand and began scaling the rocks. Higher and faster he climbed, never pausing to look back at the ocean. He could hear a roar now, and a chilling wind tore at his clothing. When he reached the top of a high rock, he clung tightly to a huge boulder while fine spray flew over him.

Finally, the wave rolled back down the beach. The sun sparkled on the wet rocks, the glistening sand, and the settling ocean waters. Alipati looked toward where his home had been. The hut was gone.

Slowly, he began climbing down and found that he still carried the Psalms leaflet. He had not prayed many times before, but now he stopped on the slippery rocks and bowed his head to tell Jesus how thankful he was.

When Alipati's father returned late in the day, he could hardly believe what he saw. "How did you ever escape being washed away?" he cried joyfully to Alipati.

"Jesus helped me," Alipati replied, and he gave his father the Psalms leaflet. "Because I read Pastor Dionisio's leaflet, Jesus helped me think of climbing the mountain."

A look of wonder crossed the father's face as he took the leaflet. For a moment, he did not speak. Then he said the words Alipati had been wanting to hear: "From now on, we'll both read all the leaflets that Pastor Dionisio brings."

Reprinted in the July 23, 2005, issue of Guide from Heaven, Please! (Washington, DC: Review and Herald® Pub. Assn., 1973).

23

Saved by a Hair

by Linda Schweitzer

This weekend was fun, wasn't it?" David asked above the music blaring on the radio. He guided the car down the steep mountain road. He and his younger sister, Sarah, were heading home after a church campout.

Sarah didn't have a chance to answer, though. David stepped on the brakes as they approached an especially sharp turn, but the car was going too fast. Sarah felt the car sliding around the corner and looked up from her book to see a tree rushing toward her.

The tires screeched as the car slid to a stop. Sarah breathed a sigh of relief. But a moment later, the rock holding the car at the face of the hill gave way.

Sarah screamed as the car raced over the edge of the cliff, tumbling down the steep hill and rolling over and over. David and Sarah were tossed about like riders on an out-of-control roller coaster.

Boom. The car finally landed at the bottom of the hill.

"Are—are you all right?" asked David as he released his

seat belt and dropped to the roof of the upside-down car.

"Get me out!" cried Sarah, who was hanging upside down, suspended by her seat belt.

David worked at getting Sarah free, but her hair was caught in the crumpled, twisted metal of the car's roof.

"I'm never riding with you again!" sobbed Sarah as she desperately tried to get out.

"Your hair is caught!"

"Just tear it!"

"Hang on. I'm working on it," said David as he tugged on her hair. Sarah's head was pulled to the side at an odd angle.

"Owww! Ouch!" screamed Sarah as a chunk of hair ripped out.

David pulled her free, and they both stumbled out of the car to survey the damage.

Sarah finally looked up at her brother and noticed blood dripping down his face. He had a small gash over his eye. He sat down as Sarah climbed back up the hill to get help.

The first car to come by was driven by the pastor of their church, who was also heading down the mountain after the church campout. Sarah waved her hands to catch his attention. He pulled over and jumped out of the car.

"What happened? Are you hurt?" Pastor Davis called as he ran up to her.

"My brother's bleeding."

"Show me," replied Pastor Davis. He waved down another church member. "Call for help!" he shouted before following Sarah down the hill.

Minutes later, the paramedics' siren blared as rescue vehicles neared the scene. Soon a police officer was directing traffic around the emergency vehicles.

"You're really fortunate that your hair got caught in the roof," an officer said to Sarah. "If it hadn't, you might not be here."

Sarah looked at the officer in amazement.

"You see," the officer said, "if your hair hadn't pulled your head to the side, a boulder would have hit your head. As it was, the rock caved in the roof pretty bad."

"Wow, and here I was upset that my hair was ripped out!"

"Your hair will grow back; your head wouldn't," the officer said.

Later, when Sarah told her mother what the officer had said, her mother hugged her tight. Sarah thought of the words Pastor Davis had said in his prayer for their family: "Let each experience in their lives, including this one, be a lesson in Your love."

Sarah knew that his prayer had already been answered. She was still alive because of God's loving care.

24

Guerrillas, Machine Guns, and God

by Diane Aguirre

'm going to fill you with holes!"

It was hard to concentrate on the words while looking down the barrels of three machine guns. I glanced into the face behind the gun—the face that had shouted the threat. It was a girl! *A girl guerrilla?* I wondered.

I was traveling back to school after Christmas vacation. But the country in which my family served as missionaries was suffering unrest. At 4:00 A.M., we'd left the orphanage where we were stationed. My father drove down the muddy jungle track into the nearest village so I could catch the bus to the capital city by 5:00 A.M.

As I joined the huddle of people waiting for the bus, everyone was talking excitedly about the guerrilla activities.

"Did you hear they bombed the communications tower in San Luis?"

"Yes, and over to the east, they took nine gringos hostage. They killed them all!"

They were talking about Americans. Both the speaker

and the other listeners eyed me with discomfort. My blond hair and tall stature shouted that I, too, was an American.

At that moment, we heard a honk and a rumble, and the two buses pulled up with a screech of brakes and shouts from the drivers. An assistant scampered up the ladder onto the roof of the first bus, and everyone quickly tossed their bags and bundles up to be stowed on the rack. My little brown suitcase looked out of place. Another assistant hustled us onto the bus, and in scarcely three minutes, the buses roared off again.

We'd jounced over potholes and rocks for barely fifteen minutes when the brakes screeched again. "Everyone out!" a bus assistant shouted. "The road is washed out. Get your bags, and walk across the mud. The buses from yesterday are waiting on the other side to go back to the city."

Bags were tossed down to nobody in particular, with each person claiming their own. I followed the other passengers through the mud to where two more buses had waited since arriving the night before.

Dawn had broken through the trees by the time we arrived, and the drivers and their assistants quickly pushed us onto the buses. I got a seat on the first bus, in the last row by the door. Three people were wedged onto each bench, and I was on the aisle. The back of the bus was extra bouncy, but it didn't hurt much because I had only about six inches of bench to land on anyway. And I couldn't bounce off because my shoulder was jammed up against the person with the aisle seat on the opposite side.

Conversation subsided, but then suddenly became agitated and excited. I stretched my neck to see what everyone was pointing at: the remains of the radio tower that had been bombed the day before. The structure was burned, twisted, and blackened, and it had collapsed.

As I repositioned myself on my seat, I thought, *Right now, we're in the middle of guerrilla territory. They could be all around us!*

Screech! Wham! The bus suddenly jolted to a stop; the other one stopping only a few feet behind us. Almost-silent screams went through the passengers packed in the bus with me: "Guerrillas!"

Out of the bushes and trees on each side of the track, they appeared like magic—shouting, cursing, and waving machine guns. "Get out of the bus! Hurry up! Come out with your hands over your head!"

The emergency door behind my right shoulder was yanked open as the machine-gun-toting masked man outside shouted orders. At that moment, the words I had heard at the bus stop echoed through my head: "They killed nine gringos." Oh, how I wished I had a hat or a mask—anything to hide my long blond hair, blue eyes, and light skin!

The people crowding the aisle of the bus jumped to the ground first. Soon I had no choice but to jump as well.

As I landed on my feet, something like a tremor went through the band of guerrillas. "Gringa!"

Three of them dashed toward me and shoved the barrels of their machine guns in my face. One shouted a threat: "I'm going to fill you with holes!"

I looked into the girl's eyes. They were like an animal's eyes, part of a contorted face. I winced as two gun barrels jabbed into me.

Lord! I cried silently.

Then I heard a calm voice inside of me say, *"Help that old woman."*

I looked behind me. In the doorway of the bus stood a

tiny, stooped, twisted old woman, staring with dismay at the ground far below. I turned my back on the guns and lifted my hands. "Venga, señora." ("Come, ma'am.")

I lifted the woman down from the bus and steadied her on her feet. She quickly scurried past the three people surrounding me and into the group of passengers guarded by a circle of guerrillas. I turned again toward the rear bus door. This time a young woman holding a baby stood in the doorway. Two small, crying children clutched at her skirt. I pulled the children loose and set them on the ground, then reached for the baby while the mother crouched and jumped down as well. Behind her appeared a man who jumped quickly, then another older woman whom I helped.

I helped one person after another out of the bus; each of them hurried to join the group on the side of the road. But always I sensed the three machine-gun-wielding guerrillas close behind me.

Finally, the last passenger appeared—another tiny older woman. I lifted her down as easily as a child, then turned to face our captors. To my surprise, all three machine guns hung limply beside them. Three sets of eyes stared at me; three mouths hung wide open.

The woman I'd just helped edged sideways toward the group standing beside the road, and I edged over with her. The guerrillas stepped aside and let us pass. I wiggled into the center of the group and hunched down a bit, trying to make myself blend in. At least I was part of the group now. My knees were literally knocking together. I had always thought that was just a figure of speech.

Suddenly, one of the guerrillas shouted, "Go down into that field! Hurry!"

We were off in a flash. Our destination was an old

banana field on a steep slope. Most of the plants had fallen over and were rotting and slippery. By now, it had started to rain, and as we stumbled down the field, we slipped and slid.

Suddenly we heard another shout. "Tierra! Tierra!" ("Ground! Ground!")

Kaboom! The bomb's explosion sent us flying through the air, then crashing, somersaulting, and sliding through the muck and rotting leaves.

So the guerrillas were telling each other to hit the ground! I suddenly realized. Their target was a nearby electrical tower, which was now a mass of twisted metal. People were sobbing, shaking, and screaming. Some were bleeding. But no one got up.

Then I heard an aircraft. It was a military plane. *What if the guerrillas start a land-to-air battle?* I thought. *We're out in a field, completely unprotected!*

The plane circled once and flew away. They had seen all the civilians but not the guerrillas, who had taken cover in the nearby foliage. As I lay there, I glanced at my watch. I wanted to know what time I would die. It was 7:30 A.M.

The children at the orphanage are praying for me right now! I thought. Every morning the entire mission campus gathered for worship at seven. After a brief devotional, at 7:25 A.M., everyone knelt down to pray for anyone who was sick, in trouble, or traveling. I suddenly realized that at that very moment, there were more than 150 people praying for me!

I was no longer afraid. My trembling and shaking stopped! "The peace of God, which transcends all understanding," flooded my soul (Philippians 4:7), and I was happy, even calm. I crawled toward those who were still hysterical with fear. "Don't be afraid," I comforted. "God will take care of us."

We were still in the field, still surrounded by desperate guerrillas. The parts of me that weren't covered by mud were still white, but I was filled with complete, overflowing peace.

We lay in the field for long minutes while the guerrillas argued, cursed, and swore at each other because their second bomb wouldn't explode. At last, they shouted their order to us: "Go back to the road!"

Once again people cried. They thought the guerrillas would kill us. We huddled together while they harangued us about the evils of organized Western government. People started edging away from me—the gringa—but I stood calm and tall because God's peace filled me completely.

Then they told us, "Go! Walk down the road to San Luis. Tell the army captain there to walk up the road single file with all his men. We want to negotiate with them. Go!"

"But why not use the buses?" someone bravely asked.

"The buses, the luggage—everything stays here. Now go!"

So we went. It was about three miles to San Luis, and it was raining, but we were joyful, thankful—alive! When we arrived, we discovered that the army captain already knew about the guerrillas. He didn't plan to walk up the road single file with his troops, only to provide target practice for the guerrillas.

Exhausted, we travelers all left and just sat down under roofs, on branches, on rocks, or beside the road.

"What are we going to do now?" I asked.

"Wait," a bus driver said.

"Wait for what?" I responded.

"Well, there will be no buses from the city until evening, and our buses are with the guerrillas. So we just wait."

A couple of hours later, the two bus drivers and their assistants stood up. To my astonishment, they started walking back up the road, laughing and joking.

"Where are they going?" someone asked.

"To get the buses," another replied.

"The buses?"

"Yes. We haven't seen any black smoke, so they haven't burned them. They can't turn them around because the road is too narrow. Besides, they don't know how to drive. One thing is certain, though. Our bus drivers will have to walk carefully because sometimes the guerrillas plant land mines in the area."

About two hours later, the buses roared into town with tooting horns and shouting drivers. The luggage packed on the roof had been looted, but we were alive!

It was a long, tiring ride into the city, but God's wonderful peace never left me. We arrived at two the next morning. As we stumbled off the buses for the last time, one of the assistants handed me my suitcase. I was shocked to see that it had not even been touched! My Bible rested on top of my folded clothes, just as I had packed it twenty-four hours earlier. God had protected my suitcase—the only "American" luggage on the entire bus!

We trudged into the bus station and waited for daybreak, when it would be safe to go out into the city. As the other weary passengers quickly fell asleep, I sat in a chair, alert, bubbling over, praising God for His grace, His deliverance, and His peace, even while I stared down the barrel of a machine gun.

25

Erica's Call for Help

by Lindsey Faith Hoyt

Erica* glanced out the back window of her friend's old, rusty Jeep. Passing by a wall of underbrush and palm trees, she marveled at the dense foliage covering the island of Saipan. She and her friend Katie were both student missionaries at the Seventh-day Adventist elementary school there and had joined three of the other student missionaries that Sunday on a trip to the beach to snorkel.

Dust billowed from the dirt road, making it impossible to keep the windows open. "I hope the water's cold!" Erica told her friends as she brushed a strand of straight brown hair out of her eyes. She ran the back of her hand over her forehead to reduce the sweat collecting there.

"I hope so, but it's getting really hot, so the shallow water will feel like a bathtub," Mark spoke from the driver's seat. "I'd be down for exploring past the reef today." Mark steered the Jeep away from a large pothole in the road.

"Didn't the locals at church advise us not to?" asked

* Names have been changed.

Erica, feeling her stomach tighten. She remembered a story she had read in the newspaper about eleven people who had drowned that year while swimming past the reef.

"Yeah, but the tide isn't strong where we'll be," Mark said. He seemed more focused on avoiding the potholes in the road than he was on Erica's question.

I don't know, Erica thought. *I'm not a strong swimmer.*

Erica went back to looking out the window. She couldn't wait to snorkel. Even if the water was warm, it would be cooler than the hot Jeep.

Five minutes later, they arrived at the beach. Once they had carried their bags down to the water's edge, they sat on a fallen palm tree to put on their snorkel gear.

With her face mask on tight, Erica waddled over to the shoreline. Mark, Cassie, Rosemary, and Katie, who were all more experienced swimmers, were already snorkeling. Stepping carefully around the sun-bleached coral mazes, Erica dipped her face below the surface of the water, looking for schools of brown-and-white clownfish, blue-banded surgeonfish, and honeycomb groupers. Today, however, there weren't many fish to see, and soon the swimmers had all snorkeled to the edge of the reef.

The five of them stood on the large porous rocks that formed a barrier at the reef's edge and breathed in the salty air. Water rolled up onto the rocks and splashed gently at their finned feet. Pointing out to the ocean, Mark suggested, "Let's swim out and do some free diving."

Cassie, Rosemary, and Katie all nodded in agreement.

Erica somberly looked at the ocean. Remembering the warning from the church members, she wondered, *Is the tide really dangerous?* From where she stood, everything looked so calm. She watched as the others jumped into the water and, not wanting to be left behind, followed suit.

Soon they were swimming in water deeper than she had ever swum in before. The gentle motion of the water made her feel safe, and she relaxed her body so she could float on her stomach and enjoy the view of the ocean floor.

The water felt cold. It felt good.

Before they knew it, a half hour had passed. Looking up, Mark told the swimmers they had drifted almost fifty yards from the reef and suggested they swim back. He and Cassie took the lead, while Katie and Rosemary followed closely behind them. Erica took up the rear.

Before they started swimming back, Rosemary turned to Erica and said, "When we get to the strongest part of the tide, do not stop swimming."

With that advice in mind, Erica focused on moving forward. She closed her eyes in order to concentrate on kicking with her legs and paddling with her arms. She noticed the current felt stronger than it had on their way out, and Erica felt grateful for her blue fins.

After a couple of minutes of swimming hard, she opened her eyes, expecting to see the reef's edge. To her dismay, the rock formations were still thirty feet away. Erica's arms started to feel heavy, and what seemed like only a short distance suddenly felt impossibly far.

Where are the others? she wondered. Looking farther, she saw that her friends had almost reached the reef. Fear began to creep into Erica's mind as she wondered whether her friends would be able to reach her if she needed help. Looking down, she realized she had been swimming over the same large coral bed the entire time she'd had her eyes closed. In fact, she was slowly losing ground to the current, which pulled her backward.

The fright in Erica's mind suddenly overwhelmed her, and she froze. Her muscles were aching. Rosemary's warning not to stop swimming rang in her ears, and she started to move again, but it felt much harder than before. *The current is too strong!*

Lifting her head, she dropped the snorkel's mouthpiece to the side of her face and shouted, "Mark! Cassie! Help!"

But the others, who were now climbing onto the rocks, didn't hear her.

"Somebody help me!" Erica called out, but this time a wave caught her by surprise, and water rolled over her unmasked face.

Sputtering from the salty mouthful, Erica panicked as the danger of the situation began to sink in. *What if Mark or Cassie can't reach me? I'll drown.*

The fatigue in Erica's arms and legs felt unbearable. The current pushed her farther out to sea with every wave.

I'm going to drown. No one will ever find me.

Facedown in the water and swimming as hard as she could, Erica prayed, *Lord, help me!*

As another wave washed over her, she heard a voice say, *"Look down."*

Scanning the ocean floor from right to left, she saw a thick rope floating twelve feet below her. On a previous trip, Mark had explained that scuba divers used the rope to navigate through the coral formations. There was only one rope that led from the reef to the beach, and there it floated, anchored with metal rings to the ocean floor.

Erica took a deep breath and dove down to grab the rope. She felt the current surge around her as her fingers grasped the thickly twisted brown cord. Quickly, she pulled herself toward the shore.

Thirty feet soon became fifteen, then five. At times, the current pushed her forward, and Erica could easily pull herself toward the reef's edge. Then the undertow would shift, and she simply held the rope, waiting.

Finally, in a gust of newfound strength, Erica pulled herself forward the remaining five feet. Letting go of the rope, she kicked to the surface. Placing her hands on the rock in front of her, she pulled herself up with the strength she had left. There she knelt in a heap on the rock, gasping for air. When she looked up, she saw Katie and Rosemary waving to her from near the shoreline.

My friends aren't going to believe what just happened! she thought.

Looking back out to the ocean, she marveled at how, right when she needed it, God had answered her prayer. In that moment, Erica thanked Him for protecting her beyond the reef.

26

A Way of Escape

by Tanneken Fros as told to Ruth Hochstetler

Angola hummed to himself as his bicycle wobbled along the bumpy dirt path through the jungle. He was headed for a little African village, where he hoped to share the gospel. For three days, he had prayed that God would help him to get there. *Lord, I believe it is my mission in life to share Your love with others. Please keep me safe.*

Arriving in the village, he began to tell the people about Jesus. Through Angola's sharing, several of them made the decision to follow Christ. A few days later, they and Angola met under a tree to start a church. Later that day, Angola left on his bicycle to ride back to his own village. He would have to hurry to make it back before dark.

Whistling as he bounced along on his bicycle, Angola gave thanks to God for the new church. A short time later, a motorcycle came toward him on the path. The driver stopped and gave Angola a warning.

"I've just managed to ride away from two lions that tried to chase me!" he said breathlessly. "You'd better be careful!"

Angola thanked the motorcyclist, then lifted his heart to God in prayer. "Dear Father, if it is Your will, please protect me." With that, he forged bravely ahead.

There was no other path for Angola to take to get to his village besides the one he was on. He hadn't traveled much farther when he saw movement in the bushes to the side of the path. *It's probably monkeys playing around*, he thought. But Angola was wrong, for suddenly, there appeared not two but *eight* lions standing directly in his path. There was nowhere to hide—only God could help him now.

Angola got off his bike, knelt down on the dirt path, and lifted his hands to heaven. "Lord, if this is to be the end of my life, I know that heaven will be my eternal home. But if You want me to keep telling people about You, please protect me from these lions!"

He waited, too afraid to open his eyes. There was only an eerie silence. Finally, he dared to look and saw four of the lions move to the right and four to the left. Angola slowly picked up his bicycle. With his heart pounding, he began walking the bike slowly between the lions. There were no growls or roars, and none of the lions moved. Angola walked a little farther, got on the bicycle, and sped off toward his home.

Suddenly, the Bible story of Daniel in the lions' den took on new meaning. How many lions there were at that time, we do not know. But this time, God had closed eight lions' mouths and provided a way of escape. By the time he was close to home, Angola was shouting praise to God for His power in protecting him. What a mighty God we serve!